MW00399595

voices on the landscape

voices on the landscape

Contemporary Iowa Poets

edited by
Michael Carey

loess hills books
farragut & parkersburg
1996

Published by: Loess Hills Books
                    an imprint of
                 Mid-Prairie Books
                 P.O. Box C
                 Parkersburg, Iowa 50665

ISBN 0-931209-64-1 cloth
ISBN 0-931209-65-x paper

acknowledgments

The editor would like to thank Phil Hey and Sandra Adelmund for their expert editorial assistance in sifting through the plethora of submitted manuscripts and for helping to weigh their comparative worth. This project could not have been as successfully accomplished without them.

A special thanks is due to Jonathan Stull for his help in encouraging those quality poets who should be included to submit and likewise to Gerald Stern for his unbridled enthusiasm, encouragement and advice on how to find many of the poets with an Iowa connection who no longer live in the state.

Most of all, the editor would like to thank all the poets who shared their work—those whose poems were accepted for this anthology and those whose poems were not. It was a joy to read them all and comforting to know that there are so many more fine poems where these came from. May the future bring you all the audience you so richly deserve.

James Autry's "Listening and Learning" was first published in *Love & Profit* (William Morrow & Co., 1991).

Marvin Bell's "White Clover" and "Trinket" are reprinted from *A Marvin Bell Reader* Copyright © Marvin Bell 1994, 1996. "The Book of the Dead Man (#48)" is printed by permission of Marvin Bell, Copyright © Marvin Bell 1996.

Robert Dana's "All We Can Do" was first published in *The Des Moines Register*. "Home" was first published in *Another Chicago Magazine*.

David Allan Evans' "Pigs" was first published in *Chariton Review*. It and "The Man in the Rendering Room" are taken from *Real and False Alarms* (BkMk Press, Kansas City, MO, 1985). All are reprinted by permission of the author, of BkMk Press, and of the curators of the University of Missouri-Kansas City.

James Galvin's "What I Believed In" was first published in *Seneca Review* and is reprinted from *Imaginary Timber* (Doubleday, 1980). Copyright © James Galvin 1975. "Real Wonder" and "More Like It" are reprinted from *Lethal Frequencies* (Copper Canyon Press, 1995). Copyright © James Galvin 1995. All are reprinted by permission of the author.

for Iowa,
may it listen to its music;
may it love what it hears

table of contents

Introduction

A few years back, I approached Bob Neymeyer of Mid-Prairie Books about establishing a special line of books dedicated to the regional Fine Arts—poetry and short stories in particular. I expected Mid-Prairie's reaction to be like other publishing houses I was in contact with, "Poetry doesn't make money. No one reads it." Well, I knew from my own experience that neither of those statements were necessarily true. Wherever I've gone, I could see with my own eyes that, more and more, people were turning to poetry for something else, some level of experience deeper and richer than what their fast-paced, electronic-media-controlled world allowed. Poetry, like a lot of things, like love perhaps, is something most people seem to take for granted in their pursuit of that which always seems more important. Yet, when something amazing or overwhelming happens in their lives—a death or a birth, marriage or a sudden shattering insight—it is only the intensity and power of poetry that comes close to containing in language the vastness they suddenly feel. As the world seems to spin faster and faster, I meet more people, who want to stop a bit, listen for and find that something small, fragile and life-affirming beating steadily inside them.

My experience with the phenomenally successful Des Moines National Poetry Festival, the University of Iowa Summer Writing Festival, and The James Hearst Celebration of Writing in Cedar Falls led me to believe that something out of the ordinary was happening. Every year I discover that the majority of post-graduate students that enroll in my summer workshops have turned to poetry because some terrible crisis in their lives made them stop and rearrange their priorities: cancer, divorce, the painful limitations of an aging body, the shackles of a successful but stifling nine-to-five job that left them yearning for more. On the other hand, these same events introduced me to many quality artists who were withering or dying inside for the lack of encouragement and support. When funding for the Arts started being slashed and trashed in Washington's most recent effort to get its fiscal house in order, I knew things were only going to get worse. It was time, I thought, to publish poetry not just as a tax write-off for huge New York-based publishing houses or through government grants to be read only by other poets or the heads of English Departments so that particular writers might get ahead in academia. For ten years, every winter, I have traveled from small town to small town across this beautiful state reading and teaching poetry. For ten years, I have been welcomed in homes and libraries and schools, on farms and in towns. Everywhere I have gone, I have gotten a warm, intelligent and enthusiastic reception. When I wrote to people, real people, and brought poetry to them, they listened, and more importantly, they *supported* it. I have found that Iowa doesn't have the highest literacy rate in the nation for nothing. In spite of the direst predictions, I decided to give back some of what Iowa has given me, in a form that might keep the blessing going. When Mid-Prairie Books said yes, Loess Hills Books was born and Bob Neymeyer and I rolled up our sleeves to get things under way.

The first tangible result of our efforts is this anthology of Iowa poets published coincidentally on the 150th anniversary of the state's birth. What we envisioned and what came about was a venue for quality, though not exclusively academic, literature—poems of every shape and character, the best of what can be found of what Iowa has to offer at this point in time. Some of the poets in this volume are among this nation's most famous and well-respected, others are known only regionally, still for some, this is their first publication. We have farmers, a lawyer, a housewife, businessmen, scientists, an ecologist, an off-shore oil technician, a social worker, a political activist, professors—the advanced and formally educated as well as those whose poetic growth was stimulated and developed solely from their own internal yearnings. All are good and worthy of support and of a wider audience.

Perhaps, because I am a farmer and spend most of my time listening to the land, my first call for manuscripts asked for work connected to Iowa's physical landscape. However, it dawned on me that most of Iowa's population lives in cities or small towns and not on farms like I do and that the city is just as important a part of Iowa's landscape as the country is. It also dawned on me that one's spiritual and emotional internal "landscape" is a real and artistically valid one. Subsequently, the definition of "landscape" widened to encompass the world each poet with an Iowa connection was coming from. What we wanted, in the end, was not a politically-oriented treatise on the environment but a representation of Iowa's best and brightest, a venue for those who have made an impact on this state's poetic "landscape" as writers and, in some cases, writing instructors, or should in the years to come. That so many of the submitted poems were written in response to aspects of Iowa's amazing physical being, pleased this editor to no end, but it was not a condition of inclusion.

Neither is this volume meant to confirm any specific definition or school of "Iowa poetry." We did not aim to recognize or foster (in farming terms) a mono-culture but to witness and help flourish the vast genetic seed bank of literary wild flowers in different stages of natural blossoming. It is our firm belief that the universe is more beautiful and more terrible than any one of us imagines, indeed more beautiful and more terrible than anyone *can* imagine. To define and limit such an infinitude would say more about the one doing the defining than it ever would about that which is being defined. In short, it is this editor's belief there are as many "types" of poetry as there are people writing it.

In the end, each of us can only speak from experience about the nature of our own definitions and our environment's effect on them. In my case, I can safely say that in my 16 years of farming, the Iowa soil has taught me a lot about language. First, I learned to compress it, because too many words can get swirled and distorted blowing across a windy field. In order to be heard, the very earth and the literal space above it forced me to learn to put a lot into a little and to wait and shoot that little through a calm moment of air. Of necessity, I had to learn to silence my small self when the great land was speaking, even though to the noisy world it didn't seem to be saying anything at all. Iowa, I learned, is not like the Rockies. It does not call attention to itself. It will not scream at you. It speaks quietly but powerfully and undeniably, as any farmer who has been able to stay in business will tell you. When you're driving on one of Iowa's highways and you hit one long curve after 40 miles of straight pavement, you *notice* that curve, you *feel* every inch of it. You learn to savor what others might take for granted. Yes, Iowa has given me a voice, but more importantly it gave me a different attitude, an attention to small things, to seemingly unimportant lives, to the musical rhythm in the very in-take and exhalation of breath. Is this not true of any good poem, or of good art in general—no matter the specific shape, fragrance or hue? This is a good quiet place, I can tell you from experience, to write and to read and to hear.

What is intended in this volume then, is something for everyone: academic and rural rustic—work that is easily accessible and work that is more artistically challenging; it is meant to be an example of the fact that whatever Iowa's voice is, it is varied, vibrant and healthy. It is my fervent wish that readers give every voice included here a moment of their lives; that they listen, gravitating first perhaps toward those voices and images that seem most familiar and comfortable, then gradually moving toward those that seem different from their own, and then finally to discover and appreciate a completely new take on the world and language. This volume is not meant to sit on a shelf. It is our fervent wish that everyone who hears these words will seek out the authors who wrote them, read their work and go to their readings. We are all neighbors here, after all, and friends—in spirit if not, yet, in fact.

What is poetry, in the end, but an expression of *spirit*? What you have before you is a snapshot of the present *soul* of Iowa. In helping to found this press I think back along the lines of my heritage, and am inspired by the hermit monks of medieval Ireland who felt it their divine calling to remain in their quiet places and copy and copy all the literature they found: the sacred and the profane, the pagan and the Christian, Biblical, classical Western and pure Celtic. When the world made it evident that it wasn't ready to accept the fruit of their endeavors, they buried their magnificently illuminated books in the woods and the fields and hid them in towers. Centuries later when the world was tired of destroying itself and wanted to peek out from the Dark Ages, their ancient light was found to guide them.

I find that eternal light still gloriously alive in the poems I read today. I want to save and disseminate each and every one of them. This is not an eminently practical undertaking, we realize. Perhaps the world is not ready, in a financially remunerative sort of way (and never quite will be), but we'll take our chances. With the publication of this anthology, Loess Hills Books dedicates itself to the fostering and preservation of all that is worthy in regional poetry and prose, to the celebration and praise of what it means to be alive—here, now, yesterday and in the years to come. Long may it be a candle in the darkness; may it never burn alone.

Michael Carey
January 2, 1996
Farragut, Iowa

Sandra Adelmund

watching the milk cows

It's probably in vain
we watch them
thinking how much
we're needed, how little
our houses mean when compared
to warm straw and lantern light.
We remember our rural beginnings:
how streets were graveled—not paved
how the errant cow—routed by flood waters—
carries with it into daybreak some secret country
we once called home. How long into the
night we'll dream them, soft and full
of milk, cooing to us, chewing their cuds,
so much trust in their eyes
it makes us squirm.

—*Sandra Adelmund*—

blackberries in iowa

What makes them
shine so? What makes them shimmer,
stir us with desire
to taste their syrup to stain
our fingers sweet
purple, makes us want
to wade into them
waist deep and breathe
breathe as though their
smell might be lilac?
And their skin transparent
at the right time shows us
the juice they carry
inside their blackberry bellies
inside their blackberry selves.
It's all so
calculated to turn us
back to our animal hungers
so we dream we are bears
raking them with claws slurping
down their purple
sucking
all the sweetness out of the world.

—*Sandra Adelmund*—

bírð clamor

I never claimed to be as intelligent
as the crow with his caw
in cold air nor did I claim
the beauty of the cardinal's incessant red
on grass below blooms of lilac. Nor was I
the sparrow who rode hollow bones toward windows
imagining them opening
onto branches. What I claimed
was the passion of the hummingbird
for flight, for ruby colors to draw
sweet drinks from. For invisibility
so that others might think I was
an accidental breeze gone by
or a twinkle in the light on a leaf. I wanted
only to fly fast and far
and leave little behind.
I wanted to feel flight
the way women want love
or men power, the suspension
of myself, the world so small
below like knickknacks, like berries
like anthills and the pull and surge
of air as I sped so breathtaking
I could forget the cardinalcrowsparrow
and live so fully on the wing
I'd be indistinguishable from leaves
or the flush of foliage. Like the creek
I'd roll forward carrying with me
a splash of light. Like daylight I'd come
upon the world with all its sorrow
take up my ruby drink and flash by
but here I am among rosebushes
with all the others around me,
a song in the center of my kind.
Only a leaf in the forest.

Gary Anderson

here

Come to the place you've always lived.
See the people you've always known.
Watch the things they do. Know you are of them.
Call. They will come.
And when they do, tell them what you have to say.
They will listen. Then they will tell you
what you've always known.

Let it be said that this is not what you wanted.
Do not say all turned out fine. It did not.
Say that you tried, and when you failed
you were brave. When you could not be brave,
you suffered silently. And when you could not be silent,
you raged. And when your rage faded,
you came here.

James A. Autry

listening and learning

There was a time I listened
to the men at the store,
thinking I could learn about farming
as they came dusty from the fields
in bib overalls and long-sleeved shirts,
their hands and faces dark red
save a white band where their straw hats sat.
They stomped their feet on the porch,
red clay dust rising to their knees,
and shook their heads as they came through the door,
always shook their heads and met the eyes
of other farmers who shook their heads
and stood at the co-cola boxes
with a Coke or Dr. Pepper or RC.
I listened about the weather
and the government
and the prices,
all of it turned against them.

Now I watch businessmen
stretch and squeeze time on planes
and in offices,
measuring their days by meetings and phone calls,
then gather in clubs
and bars and restaurants
and shake their heads and talk and talk,
about inflation and disinflation,
about the government and the deficit
and the margins
and the share fights.

After a while, it sounds the same,
farmers and businessmen,
and what I hear
is how hard it is
for them to say how much they love it.

George Barlow

the girl with tourette's

She can't help it—
the thing her brain does
without warning.
The automatic "nigger-nigger-nigger,"
the snap of her head,
the quick jut of her tongue
can happen anytime, anywhere.

So she lives
in a TV documentary
and talks about her life
while a nurse, treating new sores
on her white arms, scolds her.

Was holding her own
on the outside for a while;
was really trying; but she's back again
to care for the dolls and wigs
in her stuffed room
because this thing
causes problems in town,
at the park, at the mall:

"Can't go back to the hot dog place.
Nope. Can't get a milk shake . . .
nigger-nigger . . . nigger-nigger-nigger . . .
the guy keeps callin' security cops
'cause, ya know, the old tongue
up to the nose, ya know . . . trouble!
So I'm here . . . nigger-nigger . . .
It's um . . . it's . . . nigger . . . nigger-nigger . . .
okay, I think . . . boy oh boy . . .
so I stay here . . ."

—George Barlow—

She would stop it
if she could; would be a good girl
in the hall and in the day room;
wouldn't yank out little patches
of her hair; would leave her bandages alone;
wouldn't disturb, poor thing,
the involuntary wounds of her nation.

from **soleòaò**

3. LASSEN

From the One Yard it looks
quiet and solid
like the other two—Shasta and Ranier—
but it's not.
Nothing about its face gives it away;
men walk in and out
without looking at it.
You can't hear it from the handball courts.

The truth is muted by its paleness
and neat rows of rectangles.
Inside its seismic guts
ten million human voices—
twenty billion craggy decibels—
form one echoing drone,
one deep voice
and ten radios turned up.

Washers, dryers, showers,
card games *loud,* chess *loud,* singing *loud,*
dominoes plunked down hard
on tabletops *loud!*
Ten million metal doors slamming *loud—*
loud thoughts, *loud* feelings, *loud* naps
with crowded dreams
ranging the geography of noise.
Loud Lassen shouting from the third tier;
dark Lassen blocking out the sun;
quaking Lassen chipping the walls,
cracking the ceiling and bulging
from inside—*bellowing bellowing for release!*

4. FAMILY

The wind has caught her
in the parking lot
and pressed her pretty sundress
against her body.
Dust challenging her mascara
must yield as she glides
past the lawn and the flagpole.

In her heels and earrings,
with her short black hair
and her hot gait,
she might be the last fox—
the finest thing moving this morning.

Maybe in reverie,
in Baby-I-miss-you,
she found colors in her mirror
that were never there before.
Maybe in a dream
she found a face to wear.

There is will in her walk,
in the way she grips
her overnight case;
heat in the breeze
that kicks up her scent.

Somewhere near, in the pale belly
of the State, a man is waiting
for forty-eight hours of warmth
with a flat-out freak of nature
who makes her serious, wind-swept way
to him.

8. THE SALVATION OF IRON

Life is hard here
Nothing is funny in this hard corner
where three men pump iron
under a sun that cooks the blood
in their pecs, biceps, deltoids.

Life is heavy here
God scarred one man's face and skinned his head;
God shortened one man's leg
and cut holes in his sweatshirt;
God tatooed SOUTH BAY on one man's back.

Life is fixed here
Each man pumps and spots,
pumps and spots, shakes and blows,
pumps and spots for the common good;
each man yells out his own negative resistance.

Life is closed here
Where three souls bench fate
and curl dread
and build thick wings that will lift them
away from the mouth of Hell.

pat barlow

foR my husband

I want to embrace
the green   all shades
reflected   still
in ponds
                of collected water
in treetops
still   or blown
before there are
only sticks
        and shades of sticks
                across mounds
                        of reflecting snow
I want to lay
with you   before
all the shades

of white are still.

Marvin Bell

white clover

Once when the moon was out about three-quarters
and the fireflies who are the stars
of backyards
were out about three-quarters
and about three-fourths of all the lights
in the neighborhood
were on because people can be at home,
I took a not so innocent walk
out among the lawns,
navigating by the light of lights,
and there there were many hundreds of moons
on the lawns
where before there was only polite grass.
These were moons on long stems,
their long stems giving their greenness
to the center of each flower
and the light giving its whiteness to the tops
of the petals. I could say
it was light from stars
touched the tops of flowers and no doubt
something heavenly reaches what grows outdoors
and the heads of men who go hatless,
but I like to think we have a world
right here, and a life
that isn't death. So I don't say it's better
to be right here. I say this is where
many hundreds of core-green moons
gigantic to my eye
rose because men and women had sown green grass,
and flowered to my eye in man-made light,
and to some would be as fire in the body
and to others a light in the mind
over all their property.

trinket

I love watching the water
ooze through the crack in the fern pot,
it's a small thing

that slows time
and steadies
and gives me ideas of becoming

having nothing to do
with ambition or even reaching,
it isn't necessary at such times

to describe this,
it's no image for mean keeping,
it's no thing that small

but presence.
Other men look at the ocean,
and I do too,

though it is too many
presences for any
to absorb.

It's this other,
a little water, used, appearing
slowly around the sounds

of oxygen and small frictions,
that gives the self
the notion of the self

one is always losing
until these tiny embodiments
small enough to contain it.

the book of the dead man (#48)

Live as if you were already dead.
—Zen admonition

1. ABOUT THE DEAD MAN, ASHES AND DUST

The dead man is slag ash soot cinders grime powder
  embers flakes chips slivers snippets lava and sand.
He is fumes fog smoke and vapor.
Do not mistake the exhausted dead man for the mangled,
  dissolved or atomized.
His mark is not a blemish on the earth but a rising tide of
  consciousness.
His tracks are not the footprints in the foyer but thoughts
  brought to bear.
The letter of the dead man impedes, but the letter and the
  spirit of the dead man together animate.
The dead man is not the end but the beginning.
To conceive of the dead man is the first act of birth, incipient.
The dead man was first.
At the table, nothing more can be poured into his empty bowl.
His is the whisper that cannot be traced, the hollow that cannot
  be leveled, the absolute, the groundless ideal, the pure—in all
  respects, the substance of the honorific.
That is, everything outside the dead man is now inside the
  dead man.

2. MORE ABOUT THE DEAD MAN, ASHES AND DUST

The dead man, Ladies and Gentlemen, clears his throat.
He adopts the rhetorical posture of one to whom things happen.
He rises, he appears, he seems to be, he is.
It is the dead man's turn to toast the living, his role to
  oversee the merriment, his part to invoke the spirits and
  calculate the dusk.
He is recondite in the dun evenings, deep in the sallow dawn,
  fit for contemplation all day, he is able to sit still, he lets his
  dreams simmer in the milky overcast of a day commonly
  pictured.

—Marvin Bell—

Who but the dead man has better drawn the covers over his
head?
What better could the dead man have done to show his good
will than to keep his secrets buried?
No one hath done as much.
Consider where the dead man goes at the end of the day.
Picture his brusque exits, reconsider his gruff respects, listen
to his last words that found the nearest ear.
When the dead man clears his throat, it may be first words or
last words.
When there is no birthday, no anniversary, no jubilee, no
spree, no holiday, no one mass, meeting or service, then
naturally it is up to each person whether to go ahead or
turn back.
The dead man is 360 degrees of reasoning, three sides of a
syllogism and four sides of a simple box.

Neal Bowers

seasonal employment

The itinerant rain is back,
looking for its old job,
cozying up by making sleep
a sweeter luxury
than all the silences of snow.

We hear it first in the gutters,
a tin-pan tapping,
then a thin brush
on the windows,
a drowsy downbeat.

Soon, the whole roof
is a loose improvisation,
and we nest deeper in our pillows,
won over for another year,
the rain already busy making green.

—*Neal Bowers*—

snow angels, ltd.

Not everyone wants an angel
when we go door to door
offering our services,
a guardian under the window
or a pair of messengers.

Some prefer a white expanse,
a nothingness, some
a lawn of jumbled tracks,
and a few make their own
when no one is watching.

Ours are guaranteed distinct
through new snow and slow melts,
hollow forms filling
with a kind of purity
or vanishing to essence.

Also, we leave no footprints
to spoil the effect,
no marks at all
to lead the eye away
to guile and artifice.

Best of all is the pleasure
of seeing us fall into snow,
fanning our arms into wings,
our gaze fixed on the sky
before we rise into ourselves,
leaving behind a blessing,
the moment's embracing spirit.

small town

She comes crying, "I can't wake him,"
into the middle of the street,
her skirt a little pool of blue
when her knees give way
and the fluorescent air fixes her there
in the moments before sunrise.
Hers is the all of grief,
she the proprietor of a sudden vastness,
the yard, the trees, her own house
diminished into distance, nothing
as big as her stumbled life,
not hope, not love, not death,
not the little room where they lay down.

Paul Brooke

fourth of july fireworks

Imagine the sky
above the forest
blackened:
darkest carbon
painting a starless night.
Imagine lying
on a grassy blanket
silently, only whispers
pressing between us.
Imagine, the night
made equally
from our bodies
touching
and the ebony air.
And sleep,
coming over us
in heated waves
as we drift away
holding hands
to share
the same vivid dream
with birds
singing lullabies
in a sky of dirt.
Imagine, waking
in a ruckus
of floral explosions:
shooting star,
blue aster,
firewheel,
purple iris,
tiger lily,
snapdragon,
sunflower,
wild rose,
morning glory.

MacCanon Brown

iowa, in a ðry year

In a dry year, dust clouds roll around like dirty pots
full of topsoil and chaff. Sunny fields look brittle,
crystalline. If the ears are filled out, we will harvest
yellow topaz.

Our arms are the river valley, outstretched forward in
two banks, parallel, reaching, hands asking: a little
precipitation for the subsoil—our mother tongue, the
earth, rasps and blisters deep in the ground.

As a last resort, the wind tries to uncover bones hid in
this hill: Poweshiek, who knew prayers to the sun and
songs for rain, whose ways have dried up like streams.

Deep into my consciousness I have quarried for a primal
hymn of rain, authentic, that springs to the source.

The wind keeps blowing the dust off the page again and
again, but words to the songs and drops of rain never
appear.

the footbridge at Lynnville

Standing on the footbridge at Lynnville
I remember you.
In this exclamation of white water
and the shout I don't hear
of the child by the dam catching flash,
catching twitch, catching fish,
I recall your voice.
                    What sparks
this air, as the river's
scarred suede coat slips over
the shelf?
The picture of you in my mind,
with your arm raised high in the air
after you reached through and touched me;
raised, like these branches splashed in sunburst.

I come alive at the thought of you,
in softness and fierceness
flowing together toward a delta,
a fixity where breast joins heart
in blinding light.

Michael Carey

the holy ground

for Gilbert and Liz Barraza

In a church in Juarez, before I journeyed from El Paso to Las
Cruces and Albuquerque then on to Santa Fe, two friends,
locals, insisted that I go to Chimayo. "There's a church
there," she said, "with a hole in it you can reach down into
and pick up handfuls of dirt to rub on your hurting body.
Many have been helped and healed." He tried to make a
yearly pilgrimage. She wanted to bring their baby there as
soon as it was born. "The churchyard," she said, "was littered
with discarded wheelchairs and walkers and canes"—the
refuse of Heaven's miraculous power.

Unfortunately, snow, the interests of fellow-travelers and the
miles we had to go kept me from visiting. But I know what I
would have found. I have already found it. Even now, at
home in Iowa, I am holding it in my hands. A ground so holy
that, every so many years, I am born again from it, not
metaphorically—really: a new heart, a new brain, new skin,
new liver—everything—as I imagine it was or should be.
Again and again, day after day, year after year, molecule by
molecule, the old worn-out parts of my former self fall away
like so many discarded possessions, like once-beautiful clothes
that I have now outgrown, and I am made over. At least one
atom in my body, in every body, I have read, was once in the
body of Christ. No need to ask for new legs; I already have
them. No need to ask for new arms and hands; they are
already holding the soil that holds me, that dirties them. See
how they smudge the air till the land glitters in dust where my
name is written, where all names are written before they dis-
sipate and fall like a dark rain, like prayers said in silence, like
certain sweet songs of longing we all sing, constantly, and
only God can hear.

—*Michael Carey*—

monarchs and mowing in september

Once again,
I state the obvious
with the proviso
"I am not
making this up,"
but today, every-
where I've ridden,
on whatever tractor,
butterflies have followed
and dive-bombed around me.
Mowing the weeds
along the fence line,
on the borders
of the farms,
on the road,
under the
front yard cedars—
hundreds,
thousands,
hundreds of thousands,
who knows,
the bare arms
of the Chinese elms
were orange
with wings,
with leaves
fluttering
to the ground
and then back
up again,
floating around
my heavy body,
trying to tell
me something.
I have never
experienced
anything like their
generosity and number,

such a quiet beauty,
so insistent,
so here, so
suddenly here
knocking me
in the head,
waving before my eyes,
a beauty until now
I could only
believe was possible
bred in a faraway country,
in a field
no one has seen,
in a dream,
in a dream
it takes hope
and love
and two little eyes
to find and
a minuscule brain
and the most delicate,
trembling wings.

—Michael Carey—

iowa landscape—september 1994

for David and Pamela Clinefelter

How many swelling hills
have I sailed over,
how much
endless sky
and everywhere I turn
it's the same story
spoken differently,
each blade of grass,
each fledgling weed,
each sprouting tree
burning green,
burning white
in the black soil,
the sun's vast expanse
falling softly
through each leaf,
our one short life
covered, again
and again,
by the infinite
array of frost,
by the minute
and glittering dew,
by a huge and
simple silence,
by whatever
is open and ready
and rooted,
both near
and afar,
by whatever is
reaching out of itself
and growing
growing, growing
the whole green world round?

Robert Dana

the weeds

The weeds are what
we should have said.
And trees, all their
fine vocabularies
fallen now
to broken sentences,
to clicks and scutter.
Or sky, exhaled,
blue monosyllable,
intelligible only
in gusts of gray,
or metallic dusks,
or rain; or night's
dark wheeze
of dust and stars.

—*Robert Dana*—

all we can do

for the survivors of The Great Flood of 1993

Another rain. And another
rain. And rain's predicted.
Rain falling on rain falling
on water. Creeks and rivers
on the rise; tons of muddy
pressure pinwheeling, piling
against dike and levee, back-
pressuring dam and bank.

And where it breaks through,
it cuts nobody slack. Brown
and perfect water, perfectly
unaware of itself, flooding
over yellowed grass, stunted
corn; a couch bobbing, bucking
downstream like a bloated
steer. Live trees sliding
past. And your life like an
album of drowned photographs.

Under the unpromising sky,
we know all we can do is
curse and weep and wait;
fill sandbags, boil water,
and keep the children calm.
This. And this. Hunkered
down in the weary stink
of our boots, doing for
each other as best we can.

—*Robert Dana*—

home

The skull cracks like glass.
Then the leak and suck of the
brain, the rafters of the ribs
collapsing, and under the feet,
the foundation falling away.
West of you, we say, "Home."
"You have such a lovely home,"
she'll say. "We've so much
enjoyed visiting in your home."
I ask you to think about this.
About the collapse of the big,
beautiful blue house of daylight.

Jeanne Emmons

first frost

We bring the pots indoors.
The plants sprawl with the leggy growth
of a full season. The marigolds
gape open, bee-hungry, uncovering
all their ruffled slips.

We unfold every last sheet
to drape the tenderest vines.
The pretense of modesty alone
ought to spare their sweet skins.

Come morning, we set
the earthen pots outdoors
again and let the flowers
resume their wanton intercourse
with every flying thing.

We drag the damp linens
off the vegetables, which lie
twined around each other,
naked and unblinking
under the oblique sun.

The last fruits dawdle to maturity.
Zucchini lengthen to what end?
Potatoes quietly fatten underground.
While we bustle with the bedclothes
and talk incessantly, like Juliet's nurse,
the squash blossoms swoon open once again,
and lift their yellow crinolines
for love, for love, for love.

—*Jeanne Emmons*—

aging woman speaks of thaw

Beneath the bright sky, the snow slumps,
twenty inches of drift undercut
by rivulets of melt. The edge
of the hardpacked white
decays to slush.

The plowed banks settle and sweat
their outer white, uncovering
layer on layer of road grit
like the darkening strata
of the memory's traces.

Outside my window an icicle
salivates, lengthens on the eave.
I am suspended like that,
brittle and longing to let go.

Spruce branches bear snow
the way children trudging home with sleds
wear their sodden sleeves.
They stare at their boots and do not notice
the emaciated snowmen in their front yards,
how they shrink into themselves
and let go of their brooms.

The white poplars
sway beneath their fat, black birds,
openly, as if all along they have known
that burdensome pretense of purity
wouldn't have to be kept up forever.

Though the hair on my head grows white,
my speech blackens and diminishes
to these hard, cold utterances.
My tongue is always coming to some
shattering conclusion or other.
And I know this is how
I am going to grow old.

David Allan Evans

the acreage in iowa

in memory of William Stafford

Home was still there,
in my dream,
if I could find the street.

The tree house,
the potato garden,
the chicken shed with 15 hens,
the cornfield with two horses.
(Sometimes, out the kitchen
window we'd see them standing
close but oppositely—
the horse looking east and west.)

But when I turned at
the sign saying Lafayette,
Lafayette was not Lafayette
but a steep road to a dam
in snowy mountains.
I shifted to reverse and
turned back.

Yet there it was,
in a dream glimpse,
all of it, still:
chopping stump,
cool clods under bare feet,
wind rattling December cornstalks,
east-west-looking horse.

Home is still there,
said my dream,
if not the road going to it.

pigs

I saw the fresh cow's
head the farmer flung into
the barn for the pigs
explode them into
the shadows and land
eyes-up
between two feeders.

Minutes later, one pig,
then two, then two more
began to snuff their way
out of the shadows, toward
the head; two more,
one more, two more—
little round sharks testing
the odor of death . . .

soon the head was
at the center of a
whirlpool of feeding pigs,
then it was rising and
rolling all around—
wide eyes
coming up and going under—
not quite flying over
the barn floor but not
touching it either.

—*David Allan Evans*—

the man in the rendering room

He works his eight-hour day inside Armour's steam. The steam is his white floor and his white ceiling. It keeps belching up out of the six tank holes after he jerks open their iron lids. I rarely see him. Does the steam make him shy, an animal in fog? I just get glimpses of him.

But I can put him together. He is shirtless with a bulging chest. His back and shoulders are the color of lobster. His biceps, constantly working, are round and seamed. When I get close enough I notice he is always grinning. He never speaks. He works by himself, without breaks. I never see him puffing on a cigarette, leaning against the handles of a tankage cart, complaining about the pay or the heat.

The heat is too much for me. I can stay no longer than it takes to dump my cartload of condemned heads or kidneys or bellies. I take a deep breath before I go in. I roll my cart in fast and look around for him. I catch his finger pointing to the least-full tank. By the time I get there the lid is open and his pitchfork hands are ready. I tip my cart over the hole as the steam belches up under us, swirling and relentless, hammering my face and forehead. He is on his knees; he sticks his hands deep inside the cart, up past his elbows, up to his red shoulders and beyond, scooping, pulling, forking, jerking everything out. His back and arms and neck are matted with guts and worms. I know he is grinning; his head keeps nodding, as if he figures he can grab joy out of anything I bring him.

William Ford

attic experience

Tipton, Iowa

It's the wan hand of nostalgia
That makes you pause
And seek out your oldest flip-flops.

In the heat of deep summer
You rise into the small light
Of a gothic-windowed attic—

A mid-fifties sprawl of things
Still only partially covered,
Nothing strange expected,

Everything evened out
In the dust you'll leave yourself in
Regardless of what's touched.

Yet, strange it all is,
The oak-solid poses, unsmiling
In that rose and picket world,

The odd starched collars
Unopened to the wind,
The yellowed letters in a hand

Finer than any since
And in a language that uses time
As though in love with a sentence

That just won't end.
For a while you rock
In your father's split rocker

Pounding the baseball glove
That's cracked so badly
It won't take oil.

—William Ford—

a late song

The last birds of fall,
What do they have to sing about
Heading down into the slim light
Of the wood that has lost
Everything to the season?
We build a fire
For the short day's expectations
And the long night of sleep.

Diane Frank

planting flowers in the intuitive garden

I didn't plan where to put the irises.
The bulbs went in like a snowfall,
and two seasons later
when squawking geese shadows
flew south across the moon,
poppy seeds scattered where they fell.

As the tangled roots of warmer weather
push their way to the surface of the field,
daffodils collide with tulips.
Blueberries twist their branches
around rose petals
like a dancer who has stretched so far
beyond her natural shape
that the form has to break.
I dance in the garden at night
with pink lace climbing my ankles
and my toes bruised like blueberries.

Every day I add another flower—
columbines surprising the lattices on the porch,
shasta daisies with double rows of petals
wild as ostrich feathers or snow,
nasturtiums with edible blossoms.
Summer comes in a flood, but the wind is still breathing
with dahlias curling their leaves toward unknown colors.

I want to make love in the intuitive garden,
with peonies bent to the ground
by thunderstorms.
I want to dance in a gallery of angels
surrounded by wildflowers
and a pasture of goats and sleep.
Every day I add another flower
like the petaled surprise of love.
Every day the magenta blood of wild berries
stains my fingers and my cheeks.

James Galvin

what i've believed in

Propped on blocks, the front half of a Packard car rides the
hillside like a chip of wood on the crest of a wave. It's part of
the sawmill. That Packard engine runs it, or did. The rest, the
belt, the Belsaw carriage and blade, stands aside in disrepair.
Except for the pine seeds gophers have stashed in the
tailpipe, there's no sign of anything living. The gull-wing hood
is rusted cinnamon, latched over chrome priming cocks, one
for each cylinder. Every board in every building here was
milled on power from that old car, out of timber cut here too.
Even shingles. It's been here since 1925, winters piling onto
its forehead like a mother's hands. It's weathered them like a
son. Just because it hasn't been run since 1956 is no reason
to think it won't run now: waves have traveled thousands of
miles to give us small gifts; pine seeds have waited years to
be asked.

—*James Galvin*—

real wonder

In the stunned little interval
Between winter and spring,
Like the held gasp of surprise
Preceding real wonder,
I'm a flashlight in daylight.

Green stirs low down and shows
Through dead blond shocks of grass,
And gray aspen flowers dangle
Above old snowbanks:
I go around like a feral saint.

The timber hordes
Its meager crust of snow.
I used to walk over the hill
To visit my neighbor
About now.

Just because he was still alive
After another winter.
We'd look out the window
At the groggy meadow,
Not much to say by the end.

This year my neighbor is dead
So I walk the hill anyway.
There's his dead house.
There's his dead fence.
The timber hordes

Its meager crust of snow.
I'm a gunnysack of gravel.
I'm sudden as a gust of light.
This is just
The stunned little interval

After another winter,
The held gasp of surprise
Preceding real wonder.

more like it

1.

It's white ashes
That drift and mizzle,
Muffle and sift like snow.

Feather-ash, not snow.
Sure sign Heaven
Has burned to the ground again.

The pines
(Ah, Unanimous!)
Elect a new God.

2.

The jetstream careens
As if with a new God at the wheel.

The pines never stop praying.
They pray best in a drizzle.

The pines pray up a drought.
They pray snowdrifts and sheet lightning.

They get everything they pray for.
They get sex with the wind.

3.

Pine pollen yellows the air
Thick as smoke.
Woodgrain flames inside the pines,
Insatiable, flames
Like palms pressed together.

4.

Here in pines under ashen sky
I am. Reason is
To join my prayers
With theirs.

Mary Goose

set me free . . .

The Orange County Powwow
dancers entering the arena during the grand entry song
carrying
their individual nations' eagle-feathered staff
the Sioux Nation, the Cheyenne Nation, to name a few.

The dancers, men, women and children moving in a circle
around the drum, groups seated in the center.

Then I hear it
a sound that feels like it is coming from
a screeching eagle
hurt and in pain and falling to the Earth.

But it is only the opening guitar twangs of the
rock musician Sting in concert
next door at the outdoor amphitheater.

Singing "Free, free . . . set me free . . ."
from his song with those words from that turtle album.

"Free, free . . . set me free . . ."

The feet of many sizes and shapes
in buckskin, moosehide, tennis shoes?, moving
to the sounds of their own heartbeat and
that of the drum.

Sounds straining to be heard between
the screech of that guitar
from over that wall.

I finally smile
when I hear and feel my heart beat
silently in my body

I know which side of the wall I am standing on.

I like it here; there are no walls.

—*Mary Goose*—

earthquake

   I Breathe for silence   I try for the silence
in the place I am
I start to wake and come back from
that time in myself that I start to dream in my sleep

My voice says I just got here
let me stay
I am dragged from that playground against my will

     Who is it?

The silence breaks and
I open my eyes
to see my black and white dog looking at me
I feel my bed shaking
the carpet-covered concrete floor ripples
strangely like huge solid gray waves

I think I am really asleep and
my mother is trying to wake me up

     She is

A train rumbles through my silence
the wake-up call that says living
sometimes is on the fault line
two pieces of land fighting to meet
on one level   to become one

I look down
feeling that feeling
I only feel once a month
deep inside and below my stomach

I see red blood coming out and down
between my legs and I realize I am awake
I look up into the air

inside my six-sided box of a room
and know the full moon is now fragmented
into two pieces   my cycle ripped
forced to change into a new cycle

      NOW . . .

two weeks ahead
against my bodily will

a tight squeeze in the pit of my stomach
says
maybe it is a message from somewhere

      I am
      caught on the wrong side
      of the San Andreas fault line

I look again and see my new moon cycle,
the one ripped from my body . . .
Against my will?

I hug my dog

I know I will still have to call my mother back in Iowa
just to see if the phone lines are still connected

      I am still here
      That was the other woman, the other female
      talking to you

Jorie Graham

notes on the reality of the self

Watching the river, each handful of it closing over the next,
brown and swollen. Oaklimbs,
gnawed at by waterfilm, lifted, relifted, lapped-at all day in
this dance of non-discovery. All things are
possible. Last year's leaves, coming unstuck from shore,
rippling suddenly again with the illusion,
and carried, twirling, shiny again and fat,
towards the quick throes of another tentative
conclusion, bobbing, circling in little suctions their stiff
                                        presence
on the surface compels. Nothing is virtual.
The long brown throat of it sucking up from some faraway melt.
Expression pouring forth, all content no meaning.
The force of it and the thingness of it identical.
Spit forth, licked up, snapped where the force
exceeds the weight, clickings, pockets.
A long sigh through the land, an exhalation.
I let the dog loose in this stretch. Crocus
appear in the gassy dank leaves. Many
earth gasses, rot gasses.
I take them in, breath at a time, I put my
breath back out
onto the scented immaterial. How the invisible
roils. I see it from here and then
I see it from here. Is there a new way of looking—
valences and little hooks—inevitabilities, proba-
bilities? It flaps and slaps. Is this body the one
I know as me? How private these words? And these? Can you
smell it, brown with little froths at the rot's lips,
meanwhiles and meanwhiles thawing then growing soggy then
the filaments where leaf-matter accrued round a
pattern, a law, slipping off, precariously, bit by bit,
and flicks, and swiftnesses suddenly more water than not.

—*Jorie Graham*—

The nature of goodness the mind exhales.
I see myself. I am a widening angle of
and *nevertheless* and *this performance has rapidly*—
nailing each point and then each next right point, inter-
locking, correct, correct again, each rightness snapping loose,
floating, hook in the air, swirling, seed-down,
quick—*the evidence of the visual henceforth*—and hence-
   forth, loosening—

—*Jorie Graham*—

notes on the reality of the self

In my bushes facing the bandpractice field,
in the last light, surrounded by drumbeats, drumrolls,
there is a wind that tips the reddish leaves
exactly all one way, seizing them up from underneath,
    making them
barbarous in unison. Meanwhile the light insists they glow
where the wind churns, or no, there is a wide gold corridor
of thick insistent light, layered with golds, as if runged,
as if laid low from the edge of the sky,
in and out of which the coupling and uncoupling
limbs—the racks of limbs—the luminosities of branchings—
offspring and more offspring—roil—(except when a sudden
                      stillness reveals
an appall of pure form, pure light—
every rim clear, every leaf serrated, tongued—stripped
of the gauzy quicknesses which seemed its flesh)—but then
                  the instabilities
regroup, and the upper limbs of the tall oaks
begin to whine again with wide slappings
which seep ever-downward to my bushes—into them,
    through them—
to where the very grass makes congress with the busyness—
mutating, ridging, threshing this light from that, to no
avail—and in it all
the drumroll, rising as the ranks join in,
the wild branches letting the even drumbeats through,
ripples let through as the red branches spiral, tease,
as the crescendos of the single master-drummer
rise, and birds scatter over the field, and the wind makes each
                      thing
kneel and rise, kneel and rise, never-ending stringy
almost maternal lurching of wind
pushing into and out of the russets, magentas, incarnadines . . .
Tell me, where are the drumbeats which fully load and expand
                  each second,
bloating it up, cell-like, making it real, where are they
to go, what will *they* fill up

—Jorie Graham—

pouring forth, pouring round the subaqueous magenta bushes
which dagger the wind back down on itself,
tenderly, prudently, almost loaded down
with regret? For there is not a sound the bushes will take
from the multitude beyond them, in the field, uniformed—
(all left now on one heel) (right) (all fifty trumpets up
to the sun)—not a molecule of sound
from the tactics of this glistening beast,
forelimbs of silver (trombones, french horns)
(anointed by the day itself) expanding, retracting,
bits of red from the surrounding foliage deep
                in all the fulgid
instruments—orient—ablaze where the sound is released—
trumpeting, unfolding—
                        screeching, rolling, patterning, measuring—
scintillant beast the bushes do not know exists
as the wind beats them, beats in them, beats round them,
them in a wind that does not really even now
                        exist,
in which these knobby reddish limbs that do not sway
                by so much as an inch
its arctic course
                themselves now sway—

the visible world

I dig my hands into the absolute. The surface
                              breaks
into shingled, grassed clusters; lifts.
If I press, pick-in with fingers, pluck,
I can unfold the loam. It is tender. It is a tender
maneuver, hands making and unmaking promises.
Diggers, forgetters . . . . A series of successive single
   instances . . .
Frames of reference moving . . .
The speed of light, down here, upthrown, in my hands:
bacteria, milky roots, pilgrimages of spores, deranged
                              and rippling
mosses. What heat is this in me
that would *thaw time*, making bits of instance
                              overlap
shovel by shovelful—my present a wind blowing through
                              this culture
slogged and clutched-firm with decisions, overridings,
                              opportunities
taken? . . . If I look carefully, there in my hand, if I
                      break it apart without
crumbling: husks, mossy beginnings and endings, ruffled
                              airy loambits,
and the greasy silks of clay crushing the pinerot
                              in . . .
Erasure. Tell me something and then take it back.
Bring this pellucid moment—here on this page now
                      as on this patch
of soil, my property—bring it up to the top and out
                              of
sequence. Make it dumb again—won't you?—what
                              would it
take? Leach the humidities out, the things that will
                              insist on
making meaning. Parch it. It isn't hard: just take this

                                                    shovelful
and spread it out, deranged, a vertigo of single
                                            clots
in full sun and you can, easy, decivilize it, un-
                                    hinge it
from its plot. Upthrown like this, I think you can
                                        eventually
abstract it. Do you wish to?
Disentangled, it grows very very clear.
Even the mud, the sticky lemon-colored clay
hardens and then yields, crumbs.
I can't say what it is then, but the golden-headed
                                    hallucination,
mating, forgetting, speckling, inter-
                            locking,
will begin to be gone from it and then its glamorous
                                        veil of
echoes and muddy nostalgias will
be gone. If I touch the slender new rootings they show me
                                            how large I
am, look at these fingers—what a pilot—I touch, I press
                                        their slowest
electricity. . . . What speed is it at?
What speed am I at here, on my knees, as the sun traverses now
                                            and just begins
to touch my back. What speed where my fingers, under the
                                        dark oaks,
are suddenly touched, lit up—so white as they move, the ray for
                                            a moment
on them alone in the small wood.
White hands in the black-green glade,
opening the muddy cartoon of the present, taking the tiny roots
                                            of the moss
apart, hired hands, curiosity's small army, so white
                            in these greens—
make your revolution in the invisible temple,
make your temple in the invisible

revolution—I can't see the errands you run, hands gleaming
                              for this instant longer
like tinfoil at the bottom here of the tall
                    whispering oaks . . .
Listen, Boccioni the futurist says a galloping horse
                              has not four
legs (it has twenty)—and "at C there is no sequence
because there is no time"—and since
at lightspeed, etc. (everything is simultaneous): my hands
serrated with desires, shoved into these excavated
                                        fates
—mauve, maroons, gutters of flecking golds—
my hands are living in myriad manifestations
                            of light. . . .
"All forms of imitation are to be despised."
"All subjects previously used must be discarded."
"At last we shall rush rapidly past objectiveness". . .
Oh enslavement, will you take these hands
                    and hold them in
for a time longer? Tops of the oaks, do you see my tiny
                                golden hands
pushed, up to the wrists,
into the present? Star I can't see in daylight, young, light
                              and airy star—
I put the seed in. The beam moves on.

Dennis Hansen

cleaning out the barn

I bend to clean out the barn
and its accumulations of health.
The breezes augur well,
blowing *out* the window.
The heft in the pitchfork handle
gives me strength, and in the weighed
and balanced routine I find my pace,
lose track of time, achieve automatic, heedless
even of the proceedings of the legislators
coming from the dusty radio.
Too many rats in a box
form governments, acquire ideologies.
Forkful by forkful I rid myself
of this present mess,
down to the clean cement,
mind full only of hope,
and spreading the clean sheets of straw.

Phil Hey

daylilies

You needn't worry, John, she said,
I put some money by from selling eggs
for times like this. So she sat down that night
and wrote away to Gurney's for the starts.
In her mind, they stood in the front yard
beside the house, but by the time they came
she changed her mind. They'd go out by the road.
She'd thought of all those strangers going by,
especially in the heat of late June days,
and pondered what they'd like. Water, surely,
from the spring below the hill, or a patch of shade
beneath the cottonwood. They never stopped,
though, and so the flowers had to do.

You can imagine what he thought of that,
but a woman has to have her foolishness.
Oh, he never said a word, but sniffed each time
he drove the tractor out to work the field
across the road, and sniffed again coming back;
all those blooms and never any crop.

When the years of living scant caught up with them,
it wasn't the crops that failed, it was the loan.
Something with his health, too; he wouldn't say,
but she knew without asking where he'd gone
on that trip alone. As soon as he came back
she felt it clear through; he'd settled up
with the bank and bought a place in town.

Well, they have their story, though no one asks
to hear it. He mostly sits and rocks, outside
when it's pleasant, inside when it's not,
and gazes off in silence like you would
to see if you could see your furthest field.
She keeps busy, I hear, just like before.

It's someone else's field now, his dirt,
his corn, his tractor, his wife holding supper back.
And you couldn't tell the house, or where it was,
to see that field today. It's solid corn.
That's how they do things now. And yet out front,
year in, year out, those lilies come again.
Driving by, a person might despair
to think of that much gone, that little stayed
except a crowd of lilies that catch fire
in the corner of your eye. You'd have good reason.
But for my part, I'd wish that woman's luck
in choosing what outlasts me, and to learn
to flower in the midst of such neglect.

—Phil Hey—

at the river's edge

I want to talk about things I love:
how the trees stand next to the edge
so lush and upright, patient in the wind;
the colors of small stones just underwater;
the darting of minnows and the sudden pause
as they hang like a cloud against the current;
the way the water whispers at the shore,
cradling grains of sand always, back and forth;
and the water-strider, easy in his miracle,
walking anywhere, his feet dimpling the surface
so easy for all the rest of us to break.

—Phil Hey—

august, salad days

Just when the grass has browned off
is when the tomatoes start coming on.
The vines have been growing like snakes in a dream
and the boys tell me it's too much nitrogen,
but with a tomato plant at full throttle
there's no such thing as too much nitrogen.
Jack didn't have a beanstalk but a tomato vine.
You can imagine the giant getting lost in all those branches.
You don't have to imagine taking an ax to them.
A beggar would trade everything he owns for a live seed,
but he wouldn't have to worry. The tomato's trick
is to rot. Somehow all that corruption wipes the mortality
from the seed, tells it to be ready to grow.
Deer and horses, even pigs, can eat tomatoes
and the seed comes out ready, and surrounded by fertilizer.
What's the lesson here? Don't be afraid
when all the spring growers have had their fling.
Keep steady, put out lots of branches and soon enough
the fruit will show. Finally, let the bastards try to consume you.
If you can't go around them, go through them. Next year
they'll be gone to compost, but you'll come back fresh.

Jim Heynen

sioux center, iowa

Home of the Christian smile.
Not a center for Sioux.
The Dutch. A sub-
culture of yah's. Calvin-
istic and clean. Deep
winters. Sustained
by corn and thick
Holsteins, creamy
grins, and providential
care. Straight
furrows surround
the town. No mote,
no dike to protect it.
Only the creamery and grain
elevator, the old hatchery,
truck stops and bristling
steeples.

Do you think the people are nice?
The people are not nice.
The people are right.
Do you think the people are clean?
The people are clean.

Pictures of lonely hands praying.
Pictures of large horses.
Mosquitoes and white lawn chairs.
Miniature German Shepherds
in back car windows, their eyes
blinking the turns.

Do you think the people like baseball?
The people like baseball.
Do you think the people love?
The people love what is right.

John Deere and snowmobiles
and predestination for those

whom it hurts. Polished saddles.
Salads with whipped cream
and marshmallows. Thick
steaks.

Do you think the young people
drive in circles with new cars?
The young people
drive in circles with new cars.
The young people drive in circles
with new cars until they are aroused.
The new cars stop near cornfields
and graveyards and rock
in their tracks.

Do you think the people know the Beautiful?
A daughter in a white gown
who can play the church organ.
Do you think the people drink whiskey?
The people drink whiskey
in the next county.
Do you think the people would like you?
The people would not like you. You
are not one of them. But you
are important
where you are. God
loves those
who stay in their place.

one dead chicken

In the neighborhood where the boys lived, people went to a very strict church. It was a church that taught that people are evil, and that if they were left to themselves the whole world would turn into a cesspool. If left to themselves, they would eat each other like dogs. Or worse. As the boys understood it, rules kept people from going all out in their naturally bad ways. Rules and punishment. Maybe the punishment even more than the rules.

But obeying rules was sort of like holding your breath. You could do it for a while if you really kept your mind on it, but sooner or later *poof!* and you'd be back to your bad old self. There didn't seem to be much middle ground. What you were doing was either good, like holding your breath, or bad, like letting it all out. A few games might be in the good category if they weren't being played on Sunday and so long as everybody was being a good sport. Which, they supposed, meant not feeling bad if you were losing and not feeling good if you were winning. Almost all work was probably all good because it almost always felt bad in the doing. What was hardest to understand was why things that felt so good while they were doing them could be so bad when looked at from the point of view of having been done.

I am so disappointed that you did that.

How could anybody be disappointed in a boy doing what made him feel good? He was just being his naturally bad self. Was he supposed to hold his breath and believe some kind of rule that was the opposite of what he really was?

One day the boy who was thinking too much about good and bad caught a chicken and stuck it head-first into a gallon syrup can full of water. When the chicken was dead, he didn't ask himself, Now, why did I do that? He asked himself, What can I do with this dead wet chicken? Which meant, Where should I hide it? He buried it in the grove and then came back out into the ordinary world where nothing looked particularly good or bad.

He was supposed to feel guilty for doing something terrible like that. He didn't. He was supposed to be punished for doing something so awful. He wasn't. When he looked around, he couldn't see that he was any better or worse than anything or anybody around him. Only one thing was different now, and that was this one dead chicken. And that didn't seem to make things better or worse. It pretty much left him back where he started.

—Jim Heynen—

the great strength

Those who bulged from their shirts
like straw from tightly tied bales,
who won fistfights at the fair,
caught the greased pig, wrestled a steer,
were strong men of the plains.
But the great strength was private,
known only to old farmers
who could see the power
hidden in the face of a peddler
or farmhand, in the strangely shaped body,
pinched shoulders and spreading hips,
bent over like hybrid grain in the wind.

When the fields had been cleared,
when the last hay was stacked,
the last fence fixed,
when the cellar was sealed for winter,
always, there was the accident,
and he would be there
with jackknife or pliers or bare hands,
his strength coming out
from all its secret parts.
For a moment we knew:
a wagon set upright,
a hand pulled free from moving gears.
It was all in the wrists, or the legs,
or the eyes. Afterwards

there was no excitement at all,
and only a few saw him fade back to his body.

Betsy Snow Hickok

the blue is in the asking

And what color is the sky?
It is a blue that only pure things in the world—
cold metal in winter, a road after rain, true love,
may be compared to.
This tree, for example, knows how blue,
hefts its leaves higher and tries to hold
its wild yellow one day longer.
Squirrels know, who squall and run for trees
to be lifted. The wind knows
as you hear it rushing to stand back
like a curtain.

And what color is the sky:
there was rain where rain is impossible;
I heard it with my hands in the night.
It must have cleared everything as the clearing
of a throat can silence a room of people,
as a conductor's hand silences an orchestra,
and only then do you hear the music.
If you have ever awoken to light through a prism
you will know. It will break your heart. A thing so pure
should never be sifted.

And what color is the sky.
Ask enough times and it becomes an answer:
the blue is in the asking. Like Prayer. Pure words,
the voice of a man who, like a holy circusmaster,
can pitch his voice in a cathedral, his one voice,
and sound like many: the overtones, the voice's prism.
It takes a live room and a full heart
and there it is: perfect, ephemeral,
like a textbook containing all knowledge
that you can have only for a day.

on their billowing dresses

Ophelia says the spirits pull her toes at night
when the covers get too short.
I tell her how my sleep has been disrupted;
all signs point to the spirits, she says, my mothers unsettled
because I turn my back in sleep
to their photos above the bed.
The grim lines of their mouths suggest
they were also neglected in life.
Georgie, just a girl, is framed by the arching
willow on the photographer's backdrop,
her lacy dress as delicious as wedding cake,
her eyes direct and sure, hard to imagine
the lines on the family tree pointing away, then downward,
the inevitable sad marriage,
her womb weighted with child after child.
Ophelia pours libations to the ancestors;
certain cemeteries are more live than others
with the ghosts of those forgotten . . .
But already she has said too much
and I am left to learn the rituals
on my own. What can I place in the hands
of my ancestors, the women frozen in whatever time
the camera took them? One young, one old pose
is all I am left of each,
and I ponder the in-between,
the slow lining of the features, the outlining of the skull
over time, the lightness
above their eyes that diminishes, the white dress
traded for the gray.
I light white candles that smell of lilies,
I burn sage, I open my palms and ask what they want
and then it begins: they shoulder in
like pigeons, like angels; I feel the breeze
from their shawls around me. There are corridors
of them like spectators, all bowing to my altar.

They hold me under the elbows, they touch their palms
to mine, their whispering makes the candle flames duck
sideways then spring upward. They tell me
This is your time,
they give me defiance, and all my mothers
fly me on their billowing dresses, lifting me with their
hair ribbons, with their hands that worked the dough,
that worked the dirt. The white dresses are subterfuge,
are costumes: their breasts beneath are as hard as earth,
they feed me, this is manna, sweet girls, strong mothers:
I remember all of their names at once:
Phyllis Fall, Lillian Tierney, Georgie Robbins,
Ellie McKnight, Maria Cole, Betsy Snow.
They do not plead. They tell me
finish where we started, take our faces,
take our bodies, share our wombs—
this time we give them willingly—
and then we shall let you sleep;
learn to love our lengthening lines.

Brenda Hillman

the snakeskin

—And the world bent into the wide,
the field of beige and mild forevers
but the snake wanted something else;

I found its skin of stretchy diamonds
and picked it up, so I could keep
one of the two selves. The skin had eyes and the eyes

had skin, all papery before and afterward,
a little cellophane with dirt
around the rim—that's good;

there had been time for it to be one thing
before the world behind the world
called the snake, and the snake went—

—*Brenda Hillman*—

every life

—And right before daybreak the little owl returned:
two small solid o's,
like napkin holders.

Then the briefer, brighter o's of another bird of prey,
not a victim,
came across the field to welcome her.

Dawn has four stages. In the third,
everything chooses how much more it will become;
until then,
the door is the same color as the hinge,

poems fit into other poems, every life
fits into every life,
bright into dark, not deciding.
After that,

the wall notices the shadow pulled out of the soul,
gray as a puritan

and the brave, dreamy hyacinth starts to be seen—

could the garden have said
to the gardener, I made you grow? They were
beside one another.

Could that which was not yet
press forward in the world? It seemed for a brief time
it could—

vast fluttering

I walked with my traveler through a long system of valleys
at the end of summer
under a non-moon. Crowns
of periwinkle. Mint. Dusty laurel. The scent
of the nearly finished, about to become—

And those tiny loud berries were hardest at the end of summer
coming forward to be finished
—not having enough existence to be ripe
(yet full of crimson crimson hope)—
the white blossoms that would not fruit
were powdery at the center,
moon-powdery like the sixties, and the blossoms
came forward as trapped light.

What is the uncertain part that wants to be finished by another
What little uncertain part comes forth in thorns
each thorn hooking back to not
being a cardinal's crest
What uncertain part comes forth in thorns

(Some moths with old-lady-curtain-wings flew by)

And I loved my traveler but I feared his bright edges
the manner in which he
, looked off to the side. At mother nature.
Loved my traveler quite a lot
though he carried the past on his back—her blond changes—
and seemed at ease while I was keeping watch,
(split and puzzled and keeping watch)
he seemed at home in this bright accident,
so what was my almost compared to his being there,
my half-darkness compared to his complete light,
my local compared to his everywhere
and what was I   Was I.   (Was I)

The notion of fate pulling us sideways
Fate which traps light in the alders

Causes the vast fluttering of the supposed-to-be-there
Fate which turns young ladies into trees
and put the plague of the oak moths up that year
I loved him so outside myself I didn't fear, for several minutes!

(moths with ragged curtain wings flew by)

And the little identity owl said Fool, Fool
The archbishop of couldn't said Why, Why,
Some little nightingale-type-thing said
How previous of you

—moths with mended curtain wings flew by.

I had some boxes of noon I carried around inside
a little lit room sealed up by several dawns
I'd been reading some books on female identity
but who was I (Was I)
Had received the gifts of the new privacy
like women of my decade
Had absorbed the freckled glow of the moon in detail
But what was my little lit room
Compared to his little lit room
My sometime compared to his every single time
What were my shelves on female identity
And what was I (was I)

The problem of falling in love in this century.
The problem of it not being
natural anymore. No no not that they said no more
popular yearning. You must be in relation
to him something finished.
But I saw nature looked completely unfinished
Ellipsis and   :   :   of the cicadas
Half of an owl (maybe only one wing). Mostly
things had been omitted.

—Brenda Hillman—

Mostly I heard mostly mostly
in the Katharine Hepburn pines.

What is the part that wants to be matched by another
What part wants to be seen clear through
Doesn't want nature as the mother exactly
or wants the dark rising
colorless cobra female, the end
We walked through night till night was the poem
Night after night I felt three necessary valleys between his knuckles
Night after night, his hand stayed in my hand

An osprey stood by its possible nest.
It looked like an ace of spades standing there
sleeping. Backlit. Its neck in its pocket.
Sprigs of slightly shabby sticks it had arranged
after a casual tour of oceans.
And we loved that dark bird together,
it brooded, looking the very dawn at us,
its grief cry tucked in, for later use,
now only the gutteral R of high school French
to put itself to sleep

but so much pure creation packed around its lucky nest,
a slight, then a vast, vast fluttering;

and we loved that dark bird, together we were the bird,
he loved the center of what had already happened
and I loved what it was becoming—

so the future stretched before us as a series
of perceptions

and I saw how loving a thing beside him
I might become extra
not so less, not so unnumbered,
that loving a thing beside him I might become two—

Jan D. Hodge

old farmers

Displaced, they move to town,
walk back and forth to
empty coffee cups at Bud's cafe.

Passing our house,
they rest on the retaining wall,
linger in the ash's shade,
cast a practiced eye
over grass
where only rabbits crop.

Ron Ikan

pure shooter

His sleeves have been rolled
since the tender age of six
when a first miniature backboard
got tacked up above the door
there in his rural bedroom
for him to shoot at repeatedly
any time of the day or night,
and since then the feeling has
spread throughout his system
as these lifelong addictions will,
fixing from the third grade on
this time-honored tradition
of the true Midwestern farm boy
dangerous from the top of the key
whose folks breed Poland China
and vote straight Republican,
saddled when he was twelve
with the costly installation
of a utility pole built special
near the basket out behind the barn
giving him all the needed light
to shoot them in on those
late November evenings across
entire seasons of chill weather,
with an electric fence humming
and his basketball fairly echoing
on the smooth expansive concrete
he and a proud father poured
one long Labor Day weekend,
turning the ball over and over
in his hands a thousand times daily
there in the darkness long after supper
when all the other kids for miles
have gathered in the basement
of the old Methodist parsonage,
shooting it up even now
into orbit after soft orbit
pure as the driven snow.

—*Ron Ikan*—

mint condition

There's a familiar stranger living in our house,
down the hall where month by month his height
is marked on the frame of a door. A paper boy
and incipient alto saxophone player, he warms
to reason and rhyme, loses strength when water
comes in contact with his skin, can see through
glass enclosures like a fortune teller, is more
afraid than anything of being a child too long.
As summer twilight brings out girls who come
and call, weaving their mythologies, his thoughts
well up like winter snow inside a paperweight.
Pauper to the whims of others, he loves to be
well-liked, dreamed once of becoming a father.
King of all kaleidoscopes, master of reprisal
and alarm, surely he would settle for being a
ball player EXTRAORDINAIRE, one who hits
ropes you could hang laundry on . . . .

Karen Jobst

thoughts of winter

With only a hint of acrimony
she'll tell you
there was no way around it:
the wave and fold of her spouse
could only be compared to
the planting and harvesting
of the beans and corn,
after the last bad year
that stung the fields,
left watermarks on the tops
of his boots while he mended
fence along the north fifty,
his back to the absent green.
The sullied furls laid him open,
set him up while dawn squeezed
the dusk. His regimen of watching
the shift and stance of sky
was confession enough.
From another room she heard
his coughs of silence,
padding the distance between them,
shrinking him to a speck
in her eye,
if she let it.

Jay Johnson

ROAD

He wants to set sail
in the middle of Iowa
on the asphalt ribbon
where wild mustard
blisters the shoulders.
Past King City, The Life
of Riley RV Park.
To sail across Wild
Cat Creek he punches it.
The Porsche Turbo claws
the air. In Darling
the Winnebago is for sale.
We follow the farmer his
pail of lantern light
into the Show Me State.
We slide the sun-
roof back and drink
the morning glories
passion flowers
noxious weeds and
conversation turns
to work.
    "It's hard"
he says, "keeping it all
in the air
at the same time.
Trying to keep track.
Making forecast. The
overview of where
we need to go. I must
tell you that I was
looking forward even
though the time was
short to getting out—"
    he shifts
and puts it to the

—*Jay Johnson*—

floor. Missouri rolls
its seared tongue out
for rain and wavers
a mirage where bird
becomes fish,
fish, water, water
the long dry road
we drive on,
and drive on.

Donald Justice

elsewheres

SOUTH

The long green shutters are drawn.
Against what parades?

Closing our eyes against the sun,
We try to imagine

The darkness of an interior
Where something might still happen:

The razor lying open
On the cool marble washstand,

The drip of something—is it water?—
Upon stone floors.

NORTH

Already it is midsummer
In the Sweden of our lives.

The peasants have joined hands,
They are circling the haystacks.

We watch from the veranda.
We sit, mufflered,

Humming the tune in snatches
Under our breath.

We tremble sometimes,
Not with emotion.

WAITING ROOM

Reading the signs,
We learn what to expect—

The trains late,
The machines out of order.

We learn what it is
To stare out into space.

Great farms surround us,
Squares of a checkerboard.

Taking our places, we wait,
We wait to be moved.

ðreams of waters

1.

An odd silence
Falls as we enter
The cozy ship's-bar.

The captain, smiling,
Unfolds his spyglass
And offers to show you

The obscene shapes
Of certain islands,
Low in the offing.

I sit by in silence.

2.

People in raincoats
Stand looking out from
Ends of piers.

A fog gathers;
And little tugs,
Growing uncertain

Of their position,
Start to complain
With the deep and bearded

Voices of fathers.

3.

The season is ending.
White verandas
Curve away.

The hotel seems empty
But, once inside,
I hear a great splashing.

Behind doors
Grandfathers loll
In steaming tubs,

Huge, unblushing.

—Donald Justice—

the metamorphoses of a vampire

translated from Baudelaire

The woman, meanwhile, from her strawberry mouth—
Twisting and turning like a snake on coals,
And kneading her breasts against her corset-stays—
Let flow these words, all interfused with musk:
"My lips are moist; and I know how to make
A man forget all conscience deep in bed.
I dry all tears on my triumphant breasts
And set old men to laughing like young boys.
For those who see me naked and unveiled,
I take the place of sun, and moon, and stars!
I am, dear scholar, so well schooled in pleasure
That when I smother a man in my smooth arms
Or when I abandon to his teeth my bosom—
Shy and voluptuous, tender and robust—
Upon these cushions groaning with delight,
The impotent angels would damn themselves for me!"

When she had sucked the marrow from my bones,
And, languidly, I turned toward her intending
A love-kiss in return, I saw there only
A sort of leathery wineskin filled with pus!
I shut my eyes in a cold fright, and when
I opened them again to the good day,
Beside me lay no mannequin whose power
Seemed to have come from drinking human blood:
There trembled a confusion of old bones
Which creaked in turning like a weathervane,
Or like a signboard on an iron pole
Swung by the wind through the long winter nights.

Juliet Kaufmann

pheasant

After the others
scare us, bursting
into the wind,
you stop the sleigh.
The horses rear
and plunge, remembering
wings, wanting
us to be
lighter than air.
The dog hears her
under the snow.
I run to the drift
before he can
lift her.
She is light.
She has closed her eyes.
Before you can say *throw her*
over the fence!
she disappears,
leaving my fingers
covered with feathers.

Charlie Langton

we have met the enemy

A bull gone mad brought us early out
where dew slept along fences. Our lips blue
with cold, our courage multiplied
with each layer we'd put on against the damp,
we waited for only Jack knew what.
Jack, to calm the harried farmer, tapped his rifle.
There was no sight of what we'd come for, or anything
except silver grass and, now safely away
against the slight, phosphorescent line
of the horizon, cows, unhusbanded, steaming.
I never saw the bull when it did come,
but pieced together from the gun's report
and my imagination what I'd missed.
The bull fell with the sound of the shot
a second after blundering out of a corner
until then too barren to watch, which later
we called Nowhere. The farmer walked away
without a look. But we boys looked. Then clambered up
beside Jack in the truck and stayed unspeakably alive
to the feral morning musk evaporating
off our flannel shirts the whole quiet ride home.

—*Charlie Langton*—

stinger

    While yellow jackets slaked their thirst, we kept
plundering October, without a word
about the apples we squeezed cider from,
despite a stripped bolt, in a wooden press
"built to last a lifetime if we die soon
enough" Harold said, or about the wasps,
till you said you'd been stung already, twice.

    They were so relentlessly, recklessly
bent on drinking their fill of the amber
nectar rising in the vat, and your hand
so tolerant, I thought, of their desire,
and so achievably close, as you reached
down into that intoxicated swarm
and drowned one yellow heart in its craving.

Rustin Larson

creatures nobody recognizes

In the evening, alone together,
we eat our pauper soup.
On the radio, the music
of bowling balls rumbling
down a dark set of stairs
accompanies the excited cicadas. They rattle
until their skins burst, becoming
creatures nobody recognizes.
As the music falls asleep
into its black space, I think
of those creatures arriving into emptiness
the way a woman sings her way under
cool sheets.

I could spill my voice and burst
above your hurt glance which says
there's not enough money,
above your lips closed in a pout around the spoon,
above your eyes stubbornly holding back
their reservoir of starlight.
If I could burst through this shell
and be a boy again, I'd listen
to the rattle of cicadas. I'd pick their crisp
larval shells from the bark
of an elm. I'd ask those dried split bodies:
what does the heart become
when it opens, and how will we
know it again?

the lawn

Behind my house: a forest of sticks
leafless, crowned with gray birds.
In front of my house, a beautiful
treeless lawn inclines roundly to an abrupt
horizon, which is why there is this feeling
of endlessness. Here you really get a notion
of the shape of the world, and understand
why no one else is around. Some may think
"Oh behind that hill are railroad tracks
connecting two great cities" or "Behind that
hill is a graveyard." What they don't know
about this lawn is it's the end
of all great destinations. Sometimes at night
I feel as if I'm looking at another planet,
the grayness of dusk inhabiting the slow
cold rotation. But in the morning I'm by myself:
playing Mozart on the phonograph,
brewing tea, going to pick white violets
that rest on the thick green like disabled stars.

—*Rustin Larson*—

melons

You bought one, perfectly ripe,
but within days
little holes appeared
and it began to shrink from inside
like a consumptive.
Time after time we'd buy the sweet smelling globes
and they'd rot.
You said we had bad luck with melons.
I said we were cursed,

and so it was we wandered the earth dreaming
of the perfect incorruptible melon.
We would walk by a woman
and think of melons. We would walk by a man
with large knees and think of melons.
Even when we were spending money on clothes
we would think we were dealing out melon leaves,
thick and prickly, always leaving
a trace on our hands. Our shoes became
melon rinds, and our fingers, slivers of ripe
yellow melon. So when was it we stopped
thinking of these things? I think it was
the day in the supermarket when
you said to me, "Rus, I can't live
like this anymore!" and walked off,
leaving me to contemplate the absence of melons
and their traces, their juices and their mold.
"Why should I live like this either?" I thought,
and sat down on a crate, and weighed
my big round head in my hands.

Tom Lynner

geese

Honking half a mile up,
shifting line of crescent,
arrowhead or wave,
each outside wing beating
in new sky, the inside
working easier in the draft.

We hear the muffled clatter
behind us on the ground,
like dogs far off,
and first look back
before we see the truth
high up: the strung-together
broken necklace flying north.

—Tom Lynner—

absent

What makes me leave some group
I've just been in, and then look back,
to see I am not missed? The people
in this photograph? I started out
with them, comping along conversation's
edge. It's easy. I nod, I listen, note players,
the hand they try to play. More often,
it's one the group invisibly elects,
bestowing a grace without consent.
I feed on this, a silent meal, see
how it leads to discontent. Some
jockey for another's share, and take it,
if they can, and I escape attention
as they do. Then, when it's time to leave
and someone wants a photograph
to show whoever how they were here,
and not alone, perhaps, in some loose
sense, were loved, I make my move,
away, subtracting from the clinch.
The call goes out, the group collects,
half-hearted in its count. A hydra knot
of heads and limbs staggers in a stance,
smiles, innocent and glib, straight into time,
and this, time's frame. See. There everybody is.

Debra Marquart

riding shotgun through iowa with quest

this musician's life.
play until one,
pack up, get paid.
send the dancers
home drunk, sweaty
clinging to each other.
on the long way home
I ride shotgun with Quest
helping keep watch
over the night. our talk
turns to women and
death, what Quest calls
all things inevitable.
he is not so afraid
of the final embrace
as the moment before,
the arms stretched out
to us, the looking into
the eyes of it. in the dead
of this night, we agree
to trust it, the good faith
of this road running
beneath us. I tell him how
this place is like my home,
where every night
vapor lights burn
in yards, and every morning
farmers rise at dawn to milk
the cows. not for me
that life. in a family
of settlers, I was
the immigrant.
fixing my eye
on the horizon
setting myself to reel
madly across
this continent. flying
through Iowa, past

cornfields and silos,
the two-storied houses
our dancers have gone
to sleep in, I doze,
wake, doze, to find Quest,
hands on the wheel
trying to outdistance
the road. five a.m.
passing a farmyard
I see my father step out
to do the morning chores.
his shadow, bending
to pet the dog becomes
my brother. this is the time
of accidents, the ones
we'll never see.
we pass through
knowing that soon
the sun will show
its awful face, that soon
even our headlights
will be worthless.

wormwood

My father tells the story
he has told every day of his life,
of the woman brought from the south

where they still practiced the old ways,
when Doc Simon said there was no hope
because fluid was in both of his young lungs,

how the uncles fetched her by carriage
on the shortest day of winter,
how she dug deep under tall banks

for wormwood, a grayish-greenish
stinky weed that no one, not even
the Herefords would eat, how she

boiled milk and dropped the leaves in,
how she made a bitter soup
for him to drink. Here my father

sits back and breathes deep
wormwood's tale—little leaf,
tiny slip, smuggled through Customs

years ago inside some washerwoman's
sleeve. He has reached the border
of what she knows. What lies beyond

is unknown country, a tangled
wilderness of sheets, soaked
with sweat, cold rags pressed

to a burning forehead, prayers,
whispering over him in the night.
Beyond this point lives gossip,

hearsay, the places only the body
knows. Here my father's hands
grow wings, as if forming the story

from air, the old blue veins tracing
the slow curve of memory. *They say*
she named the fever "little fire"

and warned it to find a better place
to burn. When lost, he invents details—
the dozen eggs she took in payment

for her work—but he always keeps
the ending the same. How Doc Simon
asked about him, some weeks later

not seeing a notice of death
in the news. How Grandpa said,
Wormwood. How Doc Simon said,

That could have killed him.

Ken McCullough

where we are

for George Oppen

the cornfields   surround us
    bald road   to lowered sky
wind   eating darkness
        a chatter
of an ocean   growing
        Yet it is   alone   empty
    uprooted again
                        pungent   brittle
            to recognize   the black earth
the pull   the anchor
        fixed

            and struggling up

Respite

noon on the pipeline—
       break for lunch
             from stringing pipe
                    across a muddy creek

on the west bank
            Martin, our porky foreman
       snoozes off last night's hooch again
                  under an apple tree
                         old and fully shaped
his face covered
            by his polkadotted cap
       all but the stubbled
                        double chin
I lie back
       against the tire of the compressor
                  narrow my eyes
                         against the sun
    and sip peppermint tea
wasp
         perches on the lip
     of my thermos

I look at Martin again—

          though it be mid-September now
       the apple tree is festooned
                  with white blossoms
       and the empty field
              a riot
                       of white and purple clover
Martin himself
         in a body 20 years younger
              glows
              with a clean light
    I can smell from here

James McKean

northern lights

January, 1993

Spilling down is green light
and higher the red follows like rain
sheets at a distance,
washing thinner as if coating
the side of a glass, some
liquor distilled from the last
red currants of July.
Away from the blind lights
of the city we have driven into night
where the eye dilates
and parked no place we could
find again, the fields frozen, fences
hung with snow. The air
lays down its cold and on the shoulder
and against the car we lean back
to see wash after wash
this far south in Iowa. Arms clamped,
we lean into each other,
the only clouds our breathing,
the only light that of another day spilling over—
color thinned with water
and laid onto paper. Red and green
we say, knocking on the window at our children
huddled in the back seat,
who see the light of themselves only
and long for their beds
and morning.

quarry

No blasting now
but gentle work—the same thing
we fathers do for daughters. We bring them
one Saturday, warm for winter,
so they might get their fill of absence,
its clean lines and perfect faces.
And my first thought by the dangerous edge
is that we will leave them one day
an absence shaped like a father
or a single red leaf warmed by winter sun
and sinking through ice, the memory of itself
riding behind like a silhouette, a hand's weight
left on a shoulder, a kiss, a shadow
in the night-light, someone watching at the door.
Maybe. But explain this to daughters
who fill their hands with weeds and winter
flowers and square-stemmed mint and red hats
bobbing over fields below a house
empty and kneeling down beside this quarry
as if all played out. There's no one left
to count the crushed fingers.
The old bridge here has fallen, its limestone
abutments drifting, crossed now
only by sight. And if I read later
the limestone blocks we sit our daughters on,
tons beneath flowers and faces,
were cut from good dimension stone, the parent ledge
they call it, and I know then our daughters
will leave us, their fathers, an absence, a word
to look back into like a quarry pond
warm all summer as we watch from the edge, waiting
for them to break the surface, breath
held, shaking their hair from those clean lines,
their perfect, unmarked faces.

camp

Bemidji, Minnesota

On the back road, happy,
we bring you home from the north,
and hear you in the back seat sing
in Norwegian, explaining how
you stood with others before chairs and soup,
good bread and open faces and sang
for your hunger as you sing
now for us, vowels full of the sea and tides,
a gull echoing off a fjord's
granite walls rising steep into the light
that lasts all night all summer.
But it is late and dark here
and we live far inland before a simple horizon,
and as much as we missed you the long
drive south and east has left you
sleepy or is it the sheer weight
of language that tires you, an old world
rolling on the tongue,
replete with grandmothers
and flour-dusted aprons? So, sleep.
The fences along this road fasten
the corners of the fields and all turns
these days seem right.

Sandra McPherson

if the cardinals were like us

A FRIEND'S VOICE

Before I'm awake, the dreamlike
Courtesy could happen in fact—

The male places the sunflower seed
In his mate's bill.

I've seen it other mornings.
He'd seed a blush-red cloth, ruined

On a twig, if it were all
He had, my husband told me once . . .

When he does not come home,
I hope to wake to a plush bird,

A chant of flattery. I like it because
We do not have the vocabulary,

My daughter and I, to discuss
What's happened: the new day's

So bright you cannot see the porchlight on.

To come back to us, he rises
And his lover's cat

Claws up the bedstead to her side.
I find my bedtime book unmoved

From the sheet's smooth half,
And on my half the blood that—

As I've slept—has made this sheet as red
As it needs to be and ruined enough.

Now he's in our door.
And telling us, "Breakfast,

Eclairs from the bakery for breakfast.
Come down."

—Sandra McPherson—

alleys

For the man I'd marry I picked a white flower
Out of the dust behind a shed. The alleys
Are bare with such gifts—I'll pick up a penny

Or spots will be a dog approaching. It is
Not even a withered flower anymore,
But the dust of the first kind thing I did for him.

Later I brought in bouquets with creatures on them.
Voiceless, with increasing legs—not
The jays and doves I heard in alleys . . .

How long ago I was morning sick
In that city alley! Frightened
And leaning like a wino against the brick.

Trucks went there, and trash, and there
Was no delivered bird's egg in my path.
Now I am morning glad, all

Is pregnant outside me. I face the rabbit's
Victorious ears, the bumblebee, and mushrooms
On a fallen limb. There's not a house

Whose exit they don't call to,
Whose cries they don't keep
From heading into the street. These widths of sun . . .

A wren fusses inside a hedge; bones have been thrown
To the back of a fence. The dust
Is not all of kindness. I leave a bit

Of blue plate, do not steal the horseshoe
That perhaps I should. Who knows
Where anything is in a cycle? Alleys are behind us,

—*Sandra McPherson*—

But sunflowers fall forward into them–
As if to call for rain in the ruts. While in our house
There is the opposite. His unfinished glass of water

Appears to beg me for a flower.

—Sandra McPherson—

the firefly

Few master a form to be conspicuous in the night.
Sometimes I think I am the night,
Having nothing, not even a broken line.
The winter night across the neighborhood

Of past fireflies. Having lost even their slow
Radiance, their disconnections of someone
Pacing back and forth before a lamp,
Their teasing flight like the doubt in two voices:

Can I see you? and *Do you really see me?*
Day might see one,
Stopped, eating from the yellow ray-end
Of a dill blossom. But night after night

I am the stretch it once bit into
With hard catchable light,
Going in some direction, I never knew which
Until I saw it twice.

Jane Mead

between self and century

This is the century of the one lost shoe
at the side of the highway, century
of the old shoe curled back at the toe,
sole split, the usual mud-streaked heel.

This is the century of the big black oak
at the far end of this field of gold,
oak blurred by the air between us—
looking like a cloud of smoke, black
against the white smoke that is the sky.

* * *

I wanted to be the girl doing leg-lifts
in front of the evening news, the one
who's up on current events, but countries
I don't recognize the names of keep falling
and I'm between field and highway with the names
of those countries burning into my skull.

I'm the one who's always fasting
as if God would then come in,
the one with twigs snarled in her hair
watching a penful of pigs.
They lie in the mud shitting themselves
and squinting at me. I love them
because nothing can do *pig* as well as pig
and I am lost and do not know who I am, or if
life has anything to do with prayer.

* * *

The man who called me yellow-bird
had nothing to do with me.
He called me that because *he* wanted to fly
just as my sister called me limbs
so she would not have to love me.

But they had nothing to do with me.

There ought to be an image around here somewhere
with its back pushed up snug against that cloud,
an image to hold the world up, refusing
to shrug, refusing, even, to weep.

But this is the century of the old shoe.

* * *

There must have been something I loved once.
Some thing I made bright.

I think of the yellow curtains I made
for the kitchen of a small brown house.
A house that sat on the edge of a river.
Every morning my hands swept them open.
Every evening I closed them again.

Yes, it was the yellow checked curtains I made
so carefully—crooked to match the crooked house.

I must still be the woman who pulled curtains back.
I must be the road back into myself.

There must be something there. I loved
the motion of hands letting light in,
my own hands sweeping curtains back,
arching across the arc of the morning,
two white doves at the window, looking out
and the tide of light pouring in.

—Jane Mead—

in need of a world

Who wouldn't want a life
made real by the passage of time
or a world, at least,
made real by the mind. Something
solid and outer, though connected.

Who wouldn't want to know
for certain how to get there?

I'd like to tell you simply
how I passed this day putting tomatoes up,
or how I tied a stern cicada to a string
so I could feel the gentle tug
its flying in frantic circles made.

I'd like to show you the red
worm-shaped burn on my wrist
and in this way claim myself.

Instead I slip out of my every day—
away into the distant and lulling sound
of "once-upon-a-time-there-was-a-woman."

Will I ever find that perfect stance
of soul and mind from which sparks
a self uttering itself?
I'm always slipping between rows of corn—
through the field that rises toward this ridge
from which I like the houses for their smallness.

Here I lean against a Honey Locust,
feathery tree with its three-inch thorns,
and watch sagging strands of barbed wire
sway slightly in the wind—the clump
of brown fur hanging there, waving.

I watch the field of drying corn beyond,
and beyond that the soccer field
and rows of clean-lined condos.
I wait for the yellow light to flick on
in the white church across the valley.

Will I ever learn the way to love
the ordinary things I love to look at?

I'm always slipping away
between rows of corn, climbing
toward this ridge to think,
when really what I want is a ridge
or a lonely field on the edge of the world
of the mind. A place from which to speak
honestly to that man on the porch, a way
to greet the children who are swinging
on the edge of dusk behind chain-link fences.

But always it's either I or world.
World or I.

And when it's I I'm dreaming
on a quiet ridge that the tomatoes
ripened and, though I was missing,
a woman put an apron on and canned them.

And when it's world, it pushes me back
towards that madness of the soul
which is not a field, nor a ridge, nor a way.

the argument against us

The line of a man's neck, bent
over welding, torchlight breaking
shadows on his face, hands cracked
into a parched map of fields he has woken—
the gods wanted us.

Think of their patient preparation:
the creature who left the rocking waves behind,
crawling up on some beach, the sun
suddenly becoming clear. Small thing
abandoning water for air, crooked body
not quite fit for either world, but the one
that finally made it. Think of all the others.

Much later, spine uncurls, jaw pulls back, brow-bone
recedes, and as day breaks over the dry plain
a rebellious boy takes an upright step
where primitive birds are shrieking above him.

He did it for nothing. He did it
against all odds. Bone of wrist, twist
of tooth, angel of atoms—an infinity
of courage sorted into fact
against the shining backdrop of the world.

The line of one man's neck, bent—
torchlight breaking shadows on his face.

There was a creature who left the waves behind
and a naked child on a windy plain:
when the atom rips out into our only world
and we're carried away on a wave of hot wind
I will love them no less: they are just how much
the gods wanted us.

Jane Miller

separation

Well my Cadillac now that the hog herding has begun
          big ones spray-gunned
is this the permission we long for
          not in prose or stone but in action?
electric-prodded out of the pen backed into the bloody aisle
          pigs chew pigs' tails
whack the metal feeders charge the gate
          so it's beauty in the end we were after or serenity?
slapped on the rump shoved at the truck
          who shall not ever again find anchorage
never feared July never feared June
          every one with an inconsolable mother . . .

My ballast
          I've scratched a key along the side of a white Camaro
in hog heaven the place one finds
          community possible desirable
my legendary embankment
          I will never get over you
I cruise the high-pitched scream of the engine
          my tenderloin my tetracycline
I want only to illuminate a tiny thing in a coat
          woolen cap and rubber boots
marked by a spray of red paint
          just where our lovers die

though not admonished of your intentions in words

Soft thumps in the earth as you approach
you need comfort and food now your body
saved for the time being
trenches are dug under the wooden walls of the fort
that one may pass in and out
fiery arrows dart from the cliff across the river
men familiarly torch roofs
no sooner do you beat the fires with wet skins
then the fire rains down again
the cattle drink the rain
children's hair beaded with tears
a whippoorwill calls
a fish hawk lodges in the top of a pine
the dead live in the wild

hitherto I was prevented from observing
structures burn to the ground
these were events of a time
I went without you and came back without you
by and by the tempest spent itself
I allow that I'm not myself today
I slip my arm through yours
though no one ought to open up that country
first the settlements and claims
then the same land sold over and over
it's at this point in our history
we cannot go ahead if we value life
that turns into tribute
no longer visit my love

John Peterson

becoming prairie in dickinson county

In my mind I am able to just lie down
on the prairie sod
and be original and indigenous
concealed under butterflies
and nodding seedheads
while the air, thick with life,
moans like a man getting sleepy.

And I can be comfortable
and my skin impervious
to the horse flies, the ticks,
the red chiggers that march
singlefile up a stalk of wild rye.
Nor will I break out
in seasonal rashes, blister
under the buzzing sun,
or wrinkle and grow mold
in the smell of rain.

I will not know
my fat mammal's aversion
to the Midwest's weakening heat.

On my back I will see
the wolf spider's view
of the aster, the blazing star,
the black-eyed Susan,
and watch light weave through a scrim
of ruddy stalks
as dragonflies pair in the haze.

Rolling over, my fingers will spread and clutch deep
and be bound with every root,
runner and rhizome stitching
each prairie crumb to another.
And I will smile to the dickcissel
and the nematode alike.

—*John Peterson*—

I will be a good neighbor to the corn
but I will not encourage it.
An absurd frog green, it is obsequious
—like all fragile things—
with a straight-row sameness that disorients.

And in winter I will practice being dead,
when the wind wanders white over white
with only my teetering brown clumps
shattering infinitely across dark months,
but my secret life below and before me—
O, my meristem,
always hoping with my hope!

And in spring I will pop up
and yell surprise! in a whomp of fire.

For now in my mind
I have given up my job, my house,
and all my enemies have forgotten me,
now that I have gone to prairie.
My wife still visits;
she sees my transformation is complete
—I have grown resilient,
shabby, responsive to the faintest heartbeat
pulsing on these ragged hills.
She will know finally why,
will finally see me as lovely,
and she will know that only now
may I truly disappear from happiness.

Keith Ratzlaff

breath

But sometimes music is
just breath in the horn,
and breath is just air
in a body walking in the garden.
Sometimes the body
is like the delphiniums
that have refused all summer
to flower, but now are
blowing three indigo trumpets.

Some days things are reduced
to just resistance or contraction,
valves opening and closing:
the drowned woman's breath
walking by the ocean,
then walking away;
the lifeguard's
useless love for her.

And today it's the syrupy smell
of late phlox, the yellow pool
of ash leaves on the lawn,
the solo the maple is playing
now in the yard
holding its red notes
as if it could keep going,
like radium, half-life
after half-life, no tricks,
no cheating, nothing
held in the cheeks
or held back, just the
slow and sanguine exhale.

Dick Stahl

after the icehouse fire

Dad didn't have time to dig the ice pit
deeper that fall because the freeze
came early, and sawing his bumper crop
from the pond's lunar crust froze his brains.
He smiled when he said he'd stuffed them
inside the ice pack swelling the walls
of his hilltop icehouse. He swabbed
the only window dark with axle grease
and spilled enough sawdust on the hill
to wear snowshoes. After lightning burned
the icehouse, dad never spoke
about ice again, not even when he doused
the last curls of smoke choking the timbers.
We all knew when the summer glacier
slipped a sow's tail downhill. Dad stabbed
its white scales and tiny black worms
with his pick. He dug a tunnel
toward a deep swale, but he turned its track
hardly a twig. At night, the grinding,
like stripping the gears on his old Case,
deafened us, and by morning its claws had gouged
jagged slabs of earth. The only thing faster
in the county was talk about dad
boring holes into its back and packing
explosives. After the blast,
a wild cake chased us
into the cow barn
and crushed our house
before dropping its belly in the cellar
and starting to melt.

—*Dick Stahl*—

the man who loved cold fronts

nestled in his basement
with bees, chiggers,
and gnats in Mason jars,

courting bites like signs
to cool the hot summer
flutter of his butterfly bones,

while upstairs his wife
swatted swarms of bills striking
the kitchen table like hoppers

until his wild prediction
of a massive cold front
in August froze her profits

to zero. She snubbed
his next embrace, his fingertips
first drawing the slightest

drop in temperature.

Gerald Stern

my first kinglet

I saw my first kinglet in Iowa City
on Sunday, April twenty-second, 1984,
flying from tree to tree, and bush to bush.
She had a small yellow patch on her stomach,
a little white around her eyes. I reached
for a kiss, still dumb and silent as always. I put
a finger out for a branch and opened my hand
for a kind of clearing in the woods, a wrinkled
nest you'd call it, half inviting, half
disgusting maybe, or terrifying, a pink
and living nest. The kinglet stood there singing
"A Mighty Fortress Is Our God." She was
a pure Protestant, warbling in the woods,
confessing everything. I said goodbye,
a friend of all the Anabaptists, a friend
of all the Lutherans. I cleared my throat
and off she went for some other pink finger
and some other wrinkled palm. I started to whistle,
but only to the trees; my kinglet was gone
and her pipe was gone and her yellow crown was gone,
and I was left with only a spiral notebook
and the end of a pencil. I was good and careful,
for all I had left of the soul was in that stub,
a wobbling hunk of lead embedded in wood,
pine probably—pencils are strange—I sang
another Protestant hymn; the lead was loose
and after a minute I knew I'd just be holding
the blunt and slippery end. That was enough
for one Sunday. I thanked the trees, I thanked
the tulips with their six red tongues. I lay
another hour, another hour; I either
slept a little or thought a little. Life—
it could have been a horror, it could have been
gory and full of pain. I ate my sandwich
and waited for a signal, then I began
my own confession; I walked on the stones, I sighed
under a hemlock, I whistled under a pine,
and reached my own house almost out of breath

from walking too fast—from talking too loud—
from waving my arms and beating my palms; I was,
for five or ten minutes, one of those madmen you see
forcing their way down Broadway, reasoning with themselves
the way a squirrel does, the way a woodpecker does,
half dressed in leaf, half dressed in light, my dear face
appearing and disappearing, my heavy legs
with their shortened hamstrings tripping a little, a yard
away from my wooden steps and my rusty rail,
the thicket I lived in for two years, more or less,
Dutch on one side, American Sioux on the other,
Puerto Rican and Bronx Hasidic inside,
a thicket fit for a king or a wandering kinglet.

—Gerald Stern—

i sometimes think of the lamb

I sometimes think of the lamb when I crawl down
my flight of stairs, my back is twisted sideways
in a great arc of pain from the shoulder down
and the buttocks up. I think of the lamb through my tears
as I go down a step at a time, my left hand
squeezing the rail, my right hand holding my thigh
and lifting it up. As long as there is a lamb
I can get on my hands and knees if I have to
and walk across the floor like a limp wolf,
and I can get my body to the sink
and lift myself up to the white porcelain.
As long as there is a lamb, as long as he lives
in his brown pen or his green meadow,
as long as he kneels on the platform staring at the light,
surrounded by men and women with raised fingers,
as long as he has that little hump on his rear
and that little curve to his tail, as long as his foot
steps over the edge in terror and ignorance,
as long as he holds a cup to his own side,
as long as he is stabbed and venerated,
as long as there are hooves—and clattering—
as long as there is screaming and butchering.

lyric

I wonder who has pissed here
and stared—like me—at those wild petunias
or touched a purple leaf from that small pear tree.

Has anyone lain down here
beside those red peppers
or under those weak elm withers
standing in shame there?

Dear God of that grape,
has anyone snapped off a little curlicue
to see if it's wood or wire
or stripped the bark off those thick vines
and leaned against that broken fence?

Has anyone put some old parsley in his mouth
to see what the taste is
or lifted a rose mum to his face
to see if he'll live forever?

Meredith Stricker

coming near

The way you know your brother
catching his quick otter eye sideways.
Knowing how his hair grows a little weedy
& the tenderness you feel toward weeds.
The air alive as you walk into hickory
& oak woods, the path near home that remains
wild, even without wilderness to shelter it.
Hearing owls in daytime & the downtown whistle
where what's familiar startles you once again,
catches at you stiff & fragile like the netting
of newly leaved alder trees. *This is the way,*
migrating birds call. *This is the way.*
And in the underbrush, a box turtle
rocks like its own planet beneath
ecstatic wet leaves on the edge
of the field where deer make dusk visible.

—Meredith Stricker—

muddy ponds

quietly, rain fills
                    the hollows of elms & lilacs
as though in love
              water could become
                              even more wet with itself
          and split open
                      its own transparency.

    The fluid world
                  hovers at dusk,
  a blue figure
                  standing in the mind
                              unfinished, unowned
            fortunate & wet
                          guardian of our rain
      in a courtyard framed
                          by grapevines

    & the shape of syllables we can't yet hear.

Ann Struthers

the vegetarian's garden

The herbs of flavor, anise, six-foot dill
(a sprig of it will guard against a witch),
stalks of Chinese rhubarb, medicinal—
in equal rows. All order here. Life split
in balanced parts before he came along.
There's Homer's plain parsley, and chard, white-veined,
which Theognis loved—Aristotle fond
of red-leafed. Rabelais brought France romaine.

He brought me love and grief; he brought me seeds.
He left before the slender shoots unfurled.
He didn't stay, sweet thief, to hoe and weed;
he stole away and left me with a world
diminished, dark, bereft of cake and wine.
And now the blacksnake lives beneath the vine.

—Ann Struthers—

ice breaking up on the mississippi

The rigidities yield—like ice in March
the magic month.
                    —William Carlos Williams

This morning the ice flows aren't smooth shards
from a shattered pane, but lumpy, jagged,
white islands with hills, mountains, valleys.

A bald eagle perches
on one shaped like New Zealand.
He careens atop the impatient current,
impervious as the Case iron eagle
grasping a globe. He searches
the hills of steel-blue snow,
then lifts and hitches onto a thermal current
and writes Palmer Method ovals in the air.

Below, black brushy branches
ink their lines along the shore.
I look up from my morning coffee,
the rigidities giving way,
freeing a word here and there, a moment.

chicken dinner

My farm-wife mother keeps an ax cleft
in the chopping block. She takes her hook,
captures some naive rooster's foot, carries him
upside down towards his execution while he squawks
and twists and beats his wings, trying to peck
the hand that holds him. Whack! the feathered head
lies still—its red crown and wattles, yellow beak,
bright black eye still staring on the stained wood.
She lets the body go. It cartwheels—
from its severed neck, it paints the weeds vermillion.
Then she plunges the limp carcass into
a pail of boiling water to loosen
the feathers, pulls them off, throws them
to the wind. Inside the house
she flames paper in the black cook stove,
singes the naked body to burn away
pin feathers. Scrubs the carcass
with a stiff brown brush. Beneath
the breast bone cuts through the flesh
yanks out the blue intestines, throws
away the craw, slices the gizzard, spills
contents, strips its bitter yellow lining.
Tears the liver and heart from their pockets,
roasts in a 350 degree oven.
It's done for dinner at 12 when the men come
in from the fields. She stirs gravy, mashes
potatoes, and after all that hard work,
she smiles as sweet as milk.

Jonathan Stull

sheet lightning

When you see sheet lightning
do not listen, or wait for the air
to swell with rain,

instead, watch the clouds come
gliding down between the houses and
touch the dark clapboards in sleep.

Like so many faces of the dead
knotted together in time,
and dressed in smoky gowns of light,

the clouds signal the eye skyward
as they brush along the eaves,
and stare into the windows below.

Trust the gray faces whispering
your name beyond the glass, calling you
to waken and rise from sleep.

And only if your answer is yes
will the windows open to these angels,
their hearts pounding with thunder,
their wings beating wildly with light.

—*Jonathan Stull*—

erosion

When the sky lets go
there is a cast of light,

A shade of gray
faces the summer wind
and tumbles out of the clouds.

When the sky lets go
something besides rain,

Something flint and steel
falls through the wet curtain,
turning lakes into fire.

When the sky lets go
it is raining people, too.

Their bodies fly downward
into the widening storm,
and around the angry faces,

their hair is shooting light
out of the purple thunderheads.

The shoreline cannot hold them,
or the things of this world,
from lonely accusations.

The earth is washing away
beneath the sorrow of rainfall,

And those who have fallen
through lightning and loss,
into deepening cycles of water.

Mary Swander

heaven?

No, it's lying in a field in Iowa
staring at the heavens, stars streaking
the sky, their auras pulsing out, in.
Night of the meteor shower,
night of mosquito netting and pitched tent,
the flap open to the eastern horizon.
Hot, damp, August night when the rooster's crow
folds into its perch and the cricket's song
dives into the same pool as the whippoorwill.
Night of Augustus Caesar and St. Augustine,
Amish date night when the buggies race
home late, their wheels spinning up hill,
lanterns blinking, horses' manes flying.
Pegasus of the tall corn, Pegasus of the fat bean,
under my sleeping bag is the richest earth
on earth, and this is the night of
the Assumption of the Blessed Virgin Mary,
the blessed virgin prairie, the nightcrawlers
floating up through layers of black dirt.
What awaits? A choir of angels,
a chorus of sheep bleating out *how good
is the grass, how good is the flesh.*
How good were the stars to lead me here,
the year of the blue goat, brown duck,
the year of the squawk and coo, the loyal
dog who barked at strange men and storms.
O little town of Kalona, Hannakalona,
Kahlua Kalona, bull town, where the gardens
are ringed in cockscombs and cannas,
and down the road little girls sing hymns
outside the window of the dying man
propped with pillows near the screen.
Their voices hover above me, and are gone,
a flock escaped from the barn.
I chase them one way across the ditch,
over the hill, through the neighbor's
orchard and field. I chase them
back toward the house, corner the ram

against the fence, then Aries, Aries
is free and off through the grove
with the ewes and lambs close behind.
So bleat for the ones who never return,
the ones who last just this long,
the empty manger and stall, bleat
for the ones who come again, who ascend
in the clear air, dark night, holy night,
when sounds carry and trails of light
flit over our heads, and bleat for the moon,
the sun, the golden day when we will all lie
down in a field, nothing more to be done.

—*Mary Swander*—

the day

The day you have to stay on the other side
of the fence, teat and milk still in sight,
brimful, hanging from the belly of your nanny.
How lovely her blue fur, brown eyes,
ears, stiff and white, flicking away flies.
How perfect the curl of her tail, the sharp
tips of her horns, the split of her hooves.
How you can still feel your head butting
her bag to start the flow, then how
everything moves, tongue pressed against skin,
mouth tilting up and up again. The day began
the same with sun and corn, the rooster's crow,
a quick leap from the woodpile, but one look
into that water pail was enough, your own
face blurring. This is it, kid, you're grown,
teeth too big for baby stuff. So quit your
moans and peek through the slats
at the wild grape just a neck stretch within reach.
What you don't know, what you don't know.

cooped

The cluck, the quack, the coo,
Chanticleer's gusty *er-er-er-er-ooo*.
After a night content in boxes
or balanced on rough beams, safe
and locked away from the fox,
they long for the dawn, for the heavy
door to swing open, the plank let down.

Bantam and Cochin, they listen for
the moment I fiddle with the latch
(what a fudge) and the first thin
stream of light slips in. Leghorn
and Sultan, Blue Andalusians,
this is half the fun, to see which turkey
leaves her nest first, heads the line,

eggs snatched up while she breakfasts.
A scratch in the dirt, the hen and tom,
straw kicking up, a bug, a beak
in the pond, the puddle in the yard,
then it's back to business, hatchlings
learning their lessons at the speckled
wings of their moms, each day's venture

a little farther, each peck a direct strike.
But, oh, to be shut in, to be forced
to depend on something so human.
Crèvecoeur, crèvecoeur, weep and wail,
gobble and shriek for all the broken shells
and hearts. We must wait, wait, and remember
that this is just another night, the moon
up again. I imagine it may be this way
at the end: all huddled together, cramped,
the other's claw poking your lung,
the thirst so strong it claims your name.
Then the squeak of the hinge, and good layers
and bad, fine feathers and clipped wings,
strut, scurry and flap at once into the sun.

Thomas Swiss

the problem

I stay busy. That's not the problem. I work late,
I go to movies. But mostly, I guess, I rehearse.
And that's where I met her, where I first met

her friends—at the Ingersoll Dinner Theater.
Like sex when you know it's the last thing
you need, but you go on chasing it anyway—

that's how we got together. At first it wasn't much:
drinks and some awkward self-conscious talk
in a bar down the street. Then things escalated.

I remember I was walking her back to her car—
it must have been two or three nights later—
when she started telling me she'd had

her breasts done, and whipped up her shirt
to show me. Man! I suppose, when I think about it,
I should have seen that as some kind of clue.

But I didn't: I was too vain and needy. And her?
Worse. Calling on the phone or coming over—
I mean pretty soon my whole life was her,

and I couldn't do anything else. It was always
Listen, I have to talk, and I heard the urgency,
I heard a desperation in her voice that hooked me.

But at the theater, she was having problems, and it
wasn't only me who noticed. We were getting
toward the end of rehearsals—everybody gets kind

of loony then, anyway—and she'd be screw-
ing up her lines. Lines she'd said fine for weeks.
Like *Oh, God! That's what I love about Iowa.*

They roll up the sidewalks after dinner. That's not
a tough one, but when she got hold of it, there was
no way it was coming out right. *Lord God!,*

she'd say, *what I like about Iowa,* and then,
catching herself, she'd start over: *Oh, God!
That's what Iowa* . . . and it wasn't funny

like you might think, it wasn't like those
bloopers on TV. The cast, including me,
was getting pissed. I'd met her friends by then:

Michael, Lorna, some guy she called Tiger.
They had a special language, like friends
sometimes do. If you were being goofy,

you were "on a drive." If you were stressed
or couldn't cope, you weren't able to "fold
your napkin." And if you said or did something

that went too far, one of them would
say—usually in wide-eyed mock disbelief—
"honey, the rant runneth over." Finally,

we opened at the Ingersoll, and luck
was with us all. No flubbed lines, nobody sick,
no malfunctioning props or surprises. Even

the newspaper ran a flattering piece about us.
The last time the two of us went out, we saw
a movie the community college was showing:

The Blue Angel with Marlene Dietrich.
Remember how it starts out funny? Then
the next thing you know it's vicious,

it's sparing you nothing. And the scene
at the end—when the magician breaks an egg
over the guy's bald head so the yolk runs down

his face, and he starts crying like a rooster, *cock-
a-doodle-do!,* and the camera won't turn away.
Next to me in that big lecture hall they use

as a theater on weekends, I could feel her
shrinking, and then whispering from her seat:
Please, please, end this scene. But the camera

refused to blink: the rant runneth over. And
we both knew—even before the lights came
back on—that whatever we'd done to or kept

from each other didn't matter now. It was
done. We were free, and it was OK
to say so, if only we could find the words.

—Thomas Swiss—

the boy in the basket

Sidelined with others his age, with the third-graders
too small or too afraid of the ball to do much good
in these early innings, the boy in a basket goes unnoticed

until it's his time to bat. Then he is there (top of
the fourth, one kid on), being wheeled out by three
of his teammates. In caps and cleats, pushing his heavy,

gleaming, metal chair, they seem in no hurry to reach
the damp field, wading through the rough grass that sets
the basket rocking. Someone who loves him must have

rigged this contraption, someone who admires this boy
for working at a game he can't altogether play.
What happens when he hits the ball? Everybody's watching,

as over our heads the sun's setting, first mosquitoes
snag the air, and the broad shadows make it hard
to see exactly how he's positioned in that thing.

I'm curious. I want to know how it works, how he's able
to stand up, what supports him in the basket
and holds the basket to the chair. Are there parents here

not drawn into pity, and then, without a gap,
into thinking about their own kids? It's creepy,
comparing problems, but right now the usual concerns—

asthma, awkwardness, the extra pounds that bring on teasing—
all seem nothing. Yet trying to picture *his* life,
I have to go back thirty years—to when the son

of one of my mother's friends got hit, almost killed, by a car.
Though I saw him in his chair only twice, my mother
told me stories. What was I to understand? The usual stuff

about fortune and courage? Something American, Biblical?
When they arrive at home plate, this slow-moving foursome,
the helpers stand back, and one hands the boy

a bat, about half the usual size. Then the umpire lowers
the tee, and everything's strangely back on track:
the concession line starts moving again, the outfielders chat,

the duck that wandered into the bleachers
finds its way to the shady pond. That's when
I hear from the rows down in front a few people

shouting, *Come on, Tim!* Or is it *Tom?* I can't tell
from watching if Tim or Tom hears them, but then confidence,
like happiness, doesn't always need to be coaxed.

The kid who runs for the boy who can't—he knows this,
and waving to the cheering strangers,
heads for second as if he were that very boy.

Robert Tremmel

wading the tailwater

Saylorville, Iowa, April 1

for Dale Ross

High water
back in the saplings.
Willowy branches
poke fun at me,
pretending I am dead,
trying to convince me
they have caught my body
and are holding it
for the authorities.

But I am no fool.
I know the truth.

There are no authorities.

What they really intend
is to lull me
into a false sense
of security,
and then,
when I least expect it,
sell my corpse, my clothes,
my waders and gear
at one of the pawnshops downtown.

I decide to get them back,
ignore their game,
and pretend to be alive.
I cast out my line,
far as it will go, turn and glide over the sand, unfocus
my eyes and breathe through the gillslit of the moon.

—*Robert Tremmel*—

I reach
into that narrow light
further and further,
deeper and deeper
until nothing
can touch me.

—*Robert Tremmel*—

ouʀ last time ƒishing simmons' pond

A Father and Son Poem

The path we drove to get there
was a long and twisted one,
shot with holes and wheel ruts.
It started at George Simmons' porch
with a talk in the late afternoon,
then took us out the back gate,
past the garden, the creek,
the watermelon patch
hidden in the beanfield, then across
the pasture, winding around rocks
and washouts to the edge of the timber.

The cattle which spent each evening
browsing there in the meadow
above the pond barely looked up
as we passed through them.
Their quiet black bodies floated
across the bluestem, light and formless
as the last shadow of the last cloud
that had passed over them in the morning,
calm as the breeze we found waiting there
to lift us and carry us to the end
of our way and downhill into the trees.

* * *

I remember that last time well.
The cattle were gone when we came out,
and we were tired, muddy, thirsty,
still laughing and lugging
a bucketful of bluegills and bass
under the very first light
of a new moon we had never
seen before, the beginning
of what turned out to be a new day
into which we were about to pass,
suddenly strangers:

The tracks we made,
the words we spoke,
the wakes we raised
as we waded in
were already erased;
the unexpected lives
we were about to live
were already dawning
red, behind our eyes
even while the night
was rising.

Pat Underwood

building bridges

for my son, Scott

I watch you for a long time
as you lean over the creek,
readjusting stones and branches.
Only two small hands away
a waterfall your size
rushes through a wooden wheel
stuffed with foxtail grasses.
You bend close to hear
the whistling voice of water.
I smile at you
as you build your hand-hewn bridge.
Nearby a footpath
etched with owl feathers
grays under the slant
of afternoon sun.
You run through bluebells,
gooseberry starts, Sweet William,
follow the path to your pony.
She offers you the softness
of her Shetland nose,
her brown eyes, her flowing mane.
Quietly she follows you
back to the creek,
drinks long and smooth
from the clear spring water.
A pair of finches
shift tiny feet in high boughs
to see you finish
gathering stones and branches.
When the sun's shadow reaches
slowly through the canopy
of thick walnut stems,
I sweep you into my arms,
deeply inhaling the fragrance of love,
connecting the roots of the gooseberries.

Jan Weissmiller

solemn as the Rocking chair is

Although it could, it's just now not
defining itself through movement—
Open Arms! Lifted Heels!—
but through its steadied closeness
to the pink gladiolas.

—Jan Weissmiller—

recently widowed, you come to quiet me from a dream

White nightgown afloat
around the bend of the banister,
past the locked cedar chest
where my mother's young-girl
braids are stored,
at the corner of the long
hall to my room,
as the gauze curtains swell;
hair whiter than the lack of all color,
you shush me from the doorway—
fear and fear of the fear
that you'll touch me—
shush as the maple
leaves brush the window,
black leaves of the maple
which dawn will turn pale.

—Jan Weissmiller—

the yard's reason

The blue ground flowers, Scilla,
Siberian Violet,
had nothing to do with it.
Nor did the sidewalk, the terrace,
the red of the studio door.
—The tick of the clock, the blurred
   view through the screen from in here—
The shape of the woodshed, the trunk
of the oak, the street through the field
seen past the leafless trees,
it wasn't any of these.
Not the stone steps visible
in the dormant flower bed
or the stillness of the wind wheel.
Not the lock on the studio door.
Not the thought of your excitement
at seeing the wood duck.
Not even the wood duck.
Not the green sheen of moss
on the branch where it perched.

Mary Jane White

otheʀ nexts

I startled six young coon this morning,
a litter, six loose sleeves
of a coat I am beginning to covet.

Down they went in the ditch, brown
glimpse. I slowed. This's the curve
where I've met their number before.

These same ones? Earlier the year
they were younger, the size then to be
these here; I like to think they are.

Here's something more: last evening
a spotted fawn clambered by us,
a friend and me. We heard it breathing

first, and its hooves in gravel; it didn't
seem to notice us until it was close,
six feet nearly, before we thought

we saw *us* in its face.
The car that passed us
got to see it too, still running—

and braked so the boy in back
could tell, and we, in our excited
camaraderie say, we knew, we saw too!

In my childhood suburb, sightings of
live, wild animals were uncommon enough
I hardly believed they could exist

for me. I don't complain against my parents;
we lived near many children. I know
as a child it would be lonely living here

deep in the quiet country
where having a car
makes the difference, or being married.

Trapped, adventure-lonely there at home
I watched a weekend spate of wildlife shows—
the threatened herds and flocks of Africa,

the world's desert and polar regions
swept across our too-bluish screen.
I think now of what surprise existed once,

before any picture but a drawing,
that is now extinct. Gone out, if
I had walked up on a live, wild animal!

or would I not have seen, or ever gone,
vision uncorrected, and kept to home,
a married or an unmarried woman?

Home, I might have been as well-content
longing for faultless sight, faultless love,
and just as loath admit how easily, how very

cheaply desire rouses to meet life's next,
and then so rarely, and lazy, its other,
imagined moment.

—Mary Jane White—

walking on a field

I look in one direction
at a time. Peripheral vision's there,
but blurred in coming
to me by a small
infirmity I can't

expect to conquer once like
virginity or a mountaintop.
It's something I do
try to compensate
for—turning my head, whole

body to see. I feel a
little awkward and that is all as
I watch my friend's brisk
approach. We walk off
together; a cornstalk

turns on its pithy axis
as we come up, pass by its twirled blade-
like leaves, bent tassel
and swathed, full cob dropped
like the forefoot of a

bee, all golden-bleached. I draw
you one, but a good number—thousands
of these—remotely
like ourselves—stand
rustling intimately

in their ordered rows, each in
wry, minimal contact. Rooted, how
can they help but move
as they do, and bow
to hail, sleet, wind, and snow,

—Mary Jane White—

finally. Still, to speak of
these too sadly's to step ahead of
ourselves—up rises
the present, gentle,
mounded hill, plowed and

easily taken for
a pastoral *but* to Iowa's
flatness. The story
about that hill is:
a tractor flipped over

on a farmer and killed him
bloodily. This field's his place and his
absence—not so much
to us as to the
several people in his

house. Sad homily, sad old
earth's story, it's hard and right we see
enough to know a bit
about him, to make
a forcible entry.

ok, ok

I sit down, say
a short prayer
of thanks for
the carpeted seat
of the outhouse.
Susan, Stephen, what
an unexpected pleasure.
I will have to
tell them as much
in the morning.
Could this be *Vogue*
under the flashlight?
I could sit to
the first light
of morning, let
the door stand open.
        Something,
surely uncivilized,
the size of a badger
is moving outside,
distinctly rustling
off.
        Enough.
I know enough,
instinctively,
to know the size of
a badger when I
hear it.
Did you see it?
I didn't see
anything.
There are badgers.
We've seen badgers.
Skunk, coon, or what
I tell you,
it scared the shit
right out of me.
Ha, Ha.
Ha, Ha, Ha.

Gary J. Whitehead

new providence, iowa

for Amy Clampitt

In a town with two stores
we look at the leaning houses,
weathered and speechless
with nowhere to go but down,
and at the Cooperative looming
like the future above the roofs,
its ammonia tanks dangerous

with rust and what it holds
in store. I remember coming here
once, driven through in a long
black line. There were no houses
for rent, only acreages for sale
beyond the rails, toothless and flat
as far as the eye could see.

—Gary J. Whitehead—

waiting for crows in the snow

For almost as long as the silence
that opens across this flat land
like the hand of a waving giant,

I have been carrying myself back
to the clearing where four
roads meet to look for the crows

I noticed when first I came here.
The black shapes lifting like ash
into evening, dark against dark,

were more than I had ever seen
in one place together, as though
they had come from some solitude

too wingless to bear, and banded
for the exchange of caws that might
break the deep quiet. So I find

myself returning here without hands,
accepting what depends on silence,
the multitudes that pile into one.

Robley Wilson

blood

You told me the story of a girl
who, on safari with her father
in Africa, for the first time finds
blood staining her legs. Afraid
hungry animals on the dark plains
will be drawn to the scent,
she is frantic to stanch herself
with pieces of clothing, leaves,
anything to disavow her kinship
with predatory Nature, anything
to keep a deep secret undisclosed.
In camp, her father wonders why
she is silent; she can't explain.

This summer evening on the highway
a child's stuffed animal had broken
open: a pink teddy bear, its fluff
white as milkweed seed or ashes
sent flying up from the shoulders
by cars passing. An hour earlier
we made love, abandoning ourselves
because of your new moon, nothing
artificial between us; that special
slick passion was our own secret.
After, I would not let you bathe me.

Sometime later, under a hot shower
I watched the water flow orange
into the drain. I wondered whether
this was love itself trailing away
into the world's uncolored rivers,
or only the ordinary sloughing off
books say it is. Think of the girl
in Africa, ashamed to be a woman
for the first time, hot with fear
of her father, hating her kinships,
and as removed from my sentimental
loving as the white moon itself.

—Robley Wilson—

portraits of the wives

Think of the summer you drove with the family
West, of relentless sun in high skies, traffic
moving like a slow-motion nightmare, campers
named for dead tribes. Think of diners where
you stopped, two hundred miles since the last;
the list of eligible voters tacked up inside
a screen door, twelve names long not counting
the ones crossed off—deceased, or moved on.

Think of the rock shops, the Indian turquoise
bracelets and rings, the polished agate stones
good for luck. Think of the rivers, the Snake,
the Platte, the Yellowstone, the Powder, where
your kids raked transparent pools for pebbles
worn every bit as smooth by Nature, where you
and your wife stayed in the car with the doors
wide open and mapped the rest of the afternoon.

Think of museums. Every little town has one,
proud of its hundred years: dogged pioneers,
explorers, wagoneers—the old men with nothing
to lose, the young with everything to achieve,
shapers of rough land, architects of new life.
Here are instruments to break the earth, tame
animals, kill natives and rivals, build barns
and cabins, set posts and stretch angry wire.

Think of the wives. They are stern in sepia,
anonymous on the walls in yellowed albums
as if the West were peopled sans love, sans
passion. How difficult to forget those cold
eyes, those mouths thin as an incision where
progress cut out laughter, that hair black as
a Sioux brave's, those tough hands that held
the West above the murderous dirt of history.

Ray A. Young Bear

american flag dress as worn by isabel potato

You know, my father Willy Potato, and his cousin,
Jason Scarmark, are known throughout Iowa.
They came back from World War I as highly-
decorated heroes. Newspaper clippings
from *The Des Moines Chronicle* were kept
under glass at the Tama County courthouse.
These we were allowed to view once a year
during a field trip taken by Weeping
Willow Elementary. While the courthouse
collections were housed ten miles away,
the tarnished metals and wrinkled ribbons
always had an effect on us even when they
seemed so far away—like stars. Letters
of honor received by the "Potato Cousins"
were read to us by teachers, and we
were astounded by photographs of how
they smiled with arms interlocked years ago
amid the burning fields, twisted armor, and death.

We were told that when trouble in Northern Europe
resurfaced, the "Potato Cousins" made news again
for volunteering their services to America.
But the gallant offer was politely denied.
From this unwavering act of courage many
an immigrant heart was stirred. And so when
the teenage sons of white farmers enlisted in
record numbers from the surrounding counties,
the "Potato Cousins" were credited for instilling
a fervid sense of patriotism.
Once when a journalist asked the cousins what
drove them to defend the country, my father said:
*"A kwi ma-me ta kwi-mi ka ti ya ki ni. I ni-ye to ki-
a tta wa i-e tta i wa ji-ne me tto e me na na ki.*
We do not like to fight. Perhaps this is the way it was
for our grandfathers." The statement and its loose
translation was turned around to read:

—Ray A. Young Bear—

"We like to fight—unlike our grandfathers."
They were soon in demand at county
celebrations and state fairs.

In exchange for "gas, food, and *no* lodging,"
the heroes would don Sioux, *A tta,* war bonnets
and woolen uniforms to march in parades.
I would accompany them—not having a choice
in the matter—as reigning princess of the Annual
Black Eagle Child Field Days. On the hottest
and most humid summer days I felt sorry
for them as they led the processions in tight
combat boots while the State Pork Queen
and her rosy-cheeked court rode in automobiles.
Myself included, but on the trunk, facing backwards.
And following behind would be the King of the Hobos,
an ever-present celebrity. He sat on a tan horse next
to the town mayors and assorted dignitaries.
On the Hobo King's secret signal the half-intoxicated
men would crow like ragged roosters as they looked at
my exposed ankles and chapped shins.

Among them always would be the bald-headed
white prophet named Mark. Well-rounded and portly
in his foul-smelling buckskin and fur hats, Mark
would nervously rub his glistening forehead
by habit and produce toothpick-size rolls
of dirt. These unwanted gifts were tossed
to our feet like ritual before he would say,
"Long before there was Hitler I dreamt
of him, Willy." In disgust my father could
only grimace and joke in Indian to Jason about
the dirt toothpick-manufacturing fat man.
*"Ne ki-me ko-e be ma te si ya ni-a kwi-ko i ye-
na na tti-ke ke ne ma ki ni-ma ni-ni a bi ji-
wi ne si ji. Mo ko ma na-ke e i ki-ma na!*
As long as I've lived never have I known
anyone to be this dirty. And this is a white
person!"

The Black Eagle Child "Doughboys" were often
billed as the main attraction. The cousins would
march triumphantly to their own unique chant:
"Ma ni tta-ni a ne mi-i tti tti mo ya kwi
Germany *na i na-ma na na kwi!* This is the way
our voices will sound when we attack Germany!"
When the march paused, they expertly removed
the long, gleaming bayonets from their rifles
and placed them in the scabbards without looking.
Then they'd take turns singing war dance songs
for each other on the deerhide drum made from
a quarter of a wooden barrel.

From April to September we traveled
to the cardinal points of Iowa, from Titonka
to Corydon and beyond, camping along
picturesque cliffs of the Mississippi,
or the green rolling banks of the water-
clouded-by-a-fleeing-Culture Hero's-foot
Missouri River. Wearing an American Flag
dress I would wave to the crowd with my
red-tailed hawk fan, and I became accustomed
to the ugly, sky-reflecting marble eyes
                                    of the white children.
With blond disheveled hair they rolled over
the cobblestone streets mimicking death
from flint-tipped arrows. If they came close
enough where I could actually see my bright
reflection, I'd spit.

In the bizarre pretense, we were allied against
a common Teutonic threat, one could say I barely
justified everyone's existence and survivability—
a living, breathing Statue of Liberty . . .

Paul Zimmer

how we survive childhood

Orvil Peacher and I were fifty feet up
In the old oak when he lost his grip
And plunged crashing through branches
Toward certain, terrible damage,
But at the last possible moment
Before his wreck he managed to clutch
A limb and hang on for his dear life.

A long time Orvil dangled in silence,
Then slowly he lifted his eyes to peer
Up at me aghast in the canopy.
In the same daunting voice
He'd used to dare me high into
That venerable oak, he said,
"I'll bet you can't do that!"

milkweed

1.

    The old pod of Eli's face splits open
    And speaks, sludge in ditches
    At the corners of his mouth and eyes,
    Twigs hanging from his robe sleeves.

    He tells me, "Know where the cow pond
    Used to be? Where they bulldozed?
    The fence was just above there,
    Beside where we laid that drainpipe.

    It run down below the draw
    Where a hickory fell on the shed.
    Me and Lester drove a stake there
    In the snow, Christmas of '45,
    When we came back from the army.

    No, we didn't have no survey done,
    But we shook hands on that corner.
    It's there, by God—and it counts.
    You tell 'em Eli says so!"

2.

    I remember years before we were laying
    Drainpipe along the field road,
    A boulder dropped loose and blustered
    Down the ditch. We came spraying out
    Like a bunch of grasshoppers
    Until it finally wedged to a stop.

    When we finished jittering
    We saw it was going to take
    At least four normal men
    To horse that baby out.

But young Eli jumped down,
Strapped on and sailed it out
Of the bottom like milkweed fluff.

We shook our heads in wonder.
We thanked God for young Eli,
A man who could show you what
Was possible in this world.

—*Paul Zimmer*—

love poem

1.

Last days before first frost
we stroll out hand in hand
to see yellow sulfurs lift
in multitudes
over the fields
Flittering in ecstatic pairs
to descend
and spangle the hay

2.

Months later
trudging winter fields
in the morning sun
we see their million
rapturous spirits have risen
through layers of drift
to glitter
on the snow crust

the poets

Sandra Adelmund won the Minnesota Voices Project Poetry Competition, and her book *Aerial Studies* was published in 1994 by New Rivers Press in Minneapolis. She's the former Poetry Editor of *Iowa Woman*, and the former Assistant Editor of *Short Story*. Currently she's teaching high school English to Lakota students on the Rosebud Reservation in South Dakota after fourteen years of teaching on temporary contracts at universities and colleges in Iowa.

Gary Anderson was born in Council Bluffs and later lived in Boone and Madrid. He is a graduate of Wartburg College and Iowa State University. His poems have appeared in *Bluff City, California State Poetry Quarterly, Whetstone, Amelia, ELF* and numerous other literary magazines, as well as the baseball anthology *Mudville Diaries* (Avon Books). He received an Illinois Arts Council Award in 1996. He currently lives in suburban Chicago.

James Autry, a former Fortune 500 executive, is a poet and consultant whose work has had a significant influence on leadership thinking. He is the author of two management books, *Love and Profit: The Art of Caring Leadership* and *Life & Work: A Manager's Search for Meaning*. His two books of poetry are *Life After Mississippi* and *Nights Under a Tin Roof*. He received considerable national attention when he was one of the poets featured on Bill Moyers' series, *The Power of the Word*, on PBS. Mr. Autry is the co-founder of The Des Moines National Poetry Festival.

George Barlow is an Associate Professor of American Studies and English at Grinnell College and author of two books of poetry *Gumbo* (Doubleday, 1981), a National Poetry Series selection, and *Gabriel* (Broadside Press, 1974) and the co-editor of *About Time III: An Anthology of California Prison Writing* (William James Association, 1987). Some of the many anthologies that have included his work are: *In Search of Color Everywhere, Color: A Sampling of Contemporary African American Writing, Every Shut Eye Ain't Asleep, The Jazz Poetry Anthology, The Best of Intro* and *New American Poets of the 80's.*

pat barlow was born in Kearney, Nebraska and raised in Cicero, Illinois. Her sojourn to the San Francisco Bay Area produced two daughters and twin sons, all living happily in California. It took a Midwestern man to complete pat's karma—transplanting her back to Spirit Lake, Iowa where she now lives on the plains with her husband, Chuck, growing poems, golden retrievers and plants.

Marvin Bell grew up on rural Long Island outside New York City. He has taught at the Writers' Workshop in Iowa City since 1965. At present he divides his time between Iowa City and Port Townsend, Washington. The latest of his thirteen books are *The Book of the Dead Man* (poems) and *A Marvin Bell Reader* (selected poems, journals, memoirs and essays). He has received many literary honors including the 1994 Award in Literature from the American Academy of Arts and Letters, the Lamont Award from the Academy of American Poets, both Guggenheim and NEA fellowships, and Senior Fulbright Appointments to Yugoslavia and Australia. He was one of a group of distinguished poets to read at The White House during the Carter presidency.

Douglas E. Smith

Neal Bowers lives in Ames, Iowa with his wife Nancy, who is also a writer, and their four cats. He is author of three poetry collections, most recently *Night Vision* (BkMk Press), two critical studies of contemporary poets (both from the U. of Missouri Press), and a nonfiction book, *Words for the Taking: A Case of Plagiarism* (W.W. Norton). Recent poems have appeared in such journals as *The American Scholar, Poetry, The Hudson Review, The Sewanee Review,* and *Shenandoah*. Originally from Tennessee, he has grown, over the past two decades, to think of himself as an Iowan.

Paul Brooke spent his childhood in Treynor and Minden, Iowa and eventually moved to Ames in 1984. He received a B.S. in Biology and a M.A. in English from Iowa State University. Later he finished his Ph.D. in English from the University of Nebraska-Lincoln. In 1987 he discovered a need to write poetry when he worked near Prudhoe Bay, Alaska, as a biologist. By interacting with the land and native people in the Arctic, he began to understand his own philosophy towards nature and culture.

Francis Ford

MacCanon Brown—After 18 years in the traditional roles of an Iowa farm woman, MacCanon Brown now serves Milwaukee's homeless community and is a recipient of Progressive Milwaukee's 1995 Community Activist Award. She has been a teacher, lecturer, performer and Artist-in-the-Schools for both the Iowa and Wisconsin Arts Councils. Her poetry has appeared in numerous literary magazines and anthologies. Her third book, *The Verge of Green* is forthcoming from Pterodactyl Press.

Owen Carey

Michael Carey farms outside Farragut, Iowa with his wife Kelly and their four children Helen, Maeve, Andrew and Fionnuala. He is the author of three books of poetry *The Noise the Earth Makes, Honest Effort* and *Nishnabotna*; a teaching manual, *Poetry Starting From Scratch* and two plays *A Song In The Wilderness* and *Dear Iowa* (co-author). His work has been widely published in literary magazines across the United States, Great Britain and Ireland. He and his work have been featured recently in *The Wall Street Journal, Time, The Associated Press, World Monitor Today, The Des Moines Register, Read, Country America, Successful Farmer, Iowa Farmer Today* and Iowa Public Television's *Touchstone* and *Take One* programs.

Robert Dana was born in 1929, and recently retired after 40 years as Poet-in-Residence and Professor of English at Cornell College. Dana's work has been awarded two National Endowment Fellowships for poetry, one in 1985 and another in 1993. He received the Delmore Schwartz Memorial Poetry Award from New York University in 1989. His latest book, *Yes, Everything* (Another CHICAGO Press, 1994) has been characterized as *"quirky in its strengths, uncompromising in its pleasures."*

Jeanne Emmons has been an Iowan since 1978, when she immigrated from Texas with her husband to teach English and writing at Briar Cliff College. She is poetry editor of *The Briar Cliff Review* and author of a recently completed book of poetry, *Rootbound*. She won the *Iowa Woman* poetry competition in 1991 and the *South Coast Poetry Journal* prize in 1994. Her work has appeared in a number of literary journals, including *Cimarron Review, Prairie Schooner*, and *Nebraska Review*. She lives in Sioux City with her husband and two children.

Alan's Photography

David Allan Evans's third book of poems *Hanging Out With the Crows* was published in 1991 by BkMk Press. He and his wife Jan are co-authors of *Double Happiness: Two Lives in China* (U. of South Dakota Press in Vermillion, SD). His poems and stories have appeared widely in journals and anthologies such as *Heartland: Poets of the Midwest* and *The Norton Book of Sports*, edited by George Plimpton.

William Ford lives in Iowa City, where he currently teaches for the Distance Learning branch of Kirkwood Community College. He has also taught at the University of Iowa and at Coe, Lycoming and Southwestern Colleges. Recently his work has been nominated for the Pushcart Prize and has appeared in *Poetry, The Iowa Review, Poet & Critic, Southern Humanities Review, Tennessee Quarterly* and the jazz poetry anthology *Second Set* (Indiana U. Press). He has been a popular speaker at area colleges and gatherings sponsored by the Des Moines National Poetry Festival.

Anders Hansen

Diane Frank is the author of three books of poems, *The All Night Yemenite Cafe, Rhododendron Shedding Its Skin*, and *Isis*. A recipient of the Whiffen Poetry Prize, two Cressey Book Awards, and an NSFPS Poetry Prize, she is also a documentary scriptwriter with expertise in Eastern and Sacred Art. Currently, she lives in Fairfield, Iowa, where she directs Poets at 8:00, and teaches poetry, journal writing, and creative non-fiction workshops in the Professional Writing Program at Maharishi International University and in her living room.

James Galvin is the author of four books of poetry: *Imaginary Timber, God's Mistress, Elements* and *Lethal Frequencies*, and the prose work *The Meadow*. He has received the Nation/Discovery Award and an Academy of American Poets Prize as well as fellowships from the National Endowment for the Arts, the Ingram-Merrill Foundation and the Guggenheim Institute. He teaches occasionally at the Iowa Writers' Workshop and lives the rest of the year near Tie Siding, Wyoming.

Raan Goose

Mary Goose is of the Mesquakie and Chippewa Nations. She grew up in Des Moines but has many family connections to the Mesquakie Settlement near Tama, Iowa. The poems of hers published in this anthology were written during a two-year stay in California and came out of what she learned there about herself and the idea of finding security in an unstable environment.

Sandy Dyas

Jorie Graham is the author of five collections of poetry, as well as *The Dream of the Unified Field, Selected Poems 1974-1994*, from Ecco Press. She has won many of this nation's most prestigious awards for poetry. She lives in Iowa City with her husband and daughter and teaches at the Writers' Workshop at the University of Iowa.

Dennis Hansen is a native of northwest Iowa where he still lives, farms and studies love near the town of Emmetsburg.

Phil Hey writes and teaches writing at Briar Cliff College in Sioux City, Iowa. An Iowan and Midwesterner by choice, he grew up in Dixon, Illinois and attended Monmouth College, the University of Iowa and the University of Wisconsin. He is an editor on the staff of the *Briar Cliff Review* and *Celestial Light Press*, and has been active on the roster of the Iowa Arts Council and the Iowa Humanities Board.

Jorgen Jessen

Jim Heynen was born and raised on a farm outside Sioux Center, Iowa "in the last county in the state to get electricity" and is the author of three collections of short stories/prose poems, *The Man Who Kept Cigars in his Cap* (Graywolf, 1979), *You Know What is Right* (North Point Press, 1985) and *The One Room Schoolhouse* (Alfred Knopf, 1993); and several collections of poetry, including *A Suitable Church* (Copper Canyon, 1981). He now lives in St. Paul, Minnesota.

Betsy Snow Hickok is a graduate of the Iowa Writers' Workshop, and holds her undergraduate degree from Middlebury College in Middlebury, Vermont. For several summers she attended the Breadloaf Writers' Conference, winning a Metropolitan Life Scholarship one year to attend. She has published in *Poetry East* and the *New Virginia Review*. Originally from Vermont, she considers her home now to be Iowa, where she lives in a cottage on the Iowa River.

Brenda Hillman is the author of four books from Wesleyan University Press, *White Dress, Fortress, Death Tractates* and *Bright Existence* and of two chapbooks *Coffee 3 AM* (Penumbra Press) and *Autumn Sojourn* (EM Press). She has been on the faculty at the University of Iowa, presently teaches at St. Mary's College in Moraga, California and lives near Berkeley with her husband and daughter.

Jan D. Hodge is a Professor of English at Morningside College in Sioux City, Iowa. His poems have appeared in *Beloit Poetry Journal, Negative Capability, South Coast Poetry Journal, ELF: Eclectic Literary Forum, Nebraska English Journal, Nebraska Review*, Des Moines Art Center's *Anthology of Poetry*, and elsewhere. He has also published *Searching for the Windows*, a narrative lyric sequence, and *Things Taking Shape*, a collection of *carmina figurata*.

Ron Ikan—Born in Indiana, raised in Illinois, living in Iowa since 1965, Ron Ikan seems to be slowly moving west. It was in Iowa where he first met his wife and where his only son was born. For thirty years his poems have been written between the Mississippi and the Missouri Rivers. Whenever possible he wanders the five state area west of the Big Muddy where Crazy Horse lived, centering on the heart of the Great Plains at Bear Butte. Each time up the sacred mountain his offering for the Great Spirit is a new poem.

Karen Jobst's poems have appeared recently in *The Briar Cliff Review, Lyrical Iowa* and *The River King*. She lives in Urbandale, Iowa with her husband and two school-age daughters. In her spare time she writes poetry and helps at her children's school.

Jay Johnson has been published in various publications including the Des Moines Art Center's *Anthology of Poetry, Forty Days and Forty Nights, Iowa Woman, City View* and *Calapooya Collage*. She has been affiliated with Metro Arts as a participating artist, and on The Des Moines National Poetry Festival Committee since its inception. She has also collaborated with musicians, dancers and composers. Mother of two and now a grandmother, she is on a two-year assignment with her husband Jary in Barbados, West Indies. Her new hobby is snorkeling.

 **Donald Justice** was born in Miami, Florida and has taught at a number of universities including Syracuse, the University of Florida and for many years at the University of Iowa, in Iowa City where he now lives in retirement with his wife Jean Ross. His first book, *The Summer Anniversaries,* was the Lamont Poetry Selection for 1959. It was followed by *Night Light* (1967), *Departures* (1973), and *Selected Poems* (1979) which was awarded the Pulitzer Prize, and *The Sunset Maker* (1987). In 1992 University Press of New England published *A Donald Justice Reader* and in 1995 Knopf brought out his *New and Selected Poems.* He was the co-winner of the Bollingen prize in 1991. A distinguished member of the American Academy and Institute of Arts and Letters, Mr. Justice has received numerous grants in poetry from The Rockefeller Foundation, The Guggenheim Foundation, and the National Endowment for the Arts.

 **Juliet Kaufmann** has lived in Iowa City for twenty years. Her work has appeared in *The Chicago Review, Rochester Review, Cold Pastoral, Federation Reports, Afterimage, Lake Effect, In Two Cultures* and other publications. She is an administrator at the University of Iowa.

 **Charlie Langton** lives in Decorah, Iowa, where he works at Vesterheim Norwegian-American Museum. His poetry has appeared in various literary journals. He also assists in the publication of *Trapeze,* the Decorah-based quarterly of arts and ideas.

Rustin Larson was born in Des Moines, Iowa. He was educated in Iowa and later earned an M.F.A. from Vermont College of Norwich University. He is currently serving as a Poet-in-the-Schools through the Iowa Arts Council. His poetry has appeared in numerous publications including, *The New Yorker, America, Poetry East, Cimarron Review* and *Boundary 2. Loving the Good Driver,* published by Mellen Poetry Press in 1996, is his first book. He lives in southeast Iowa with his wife, Caroline and their three daughters, Katharine, Sarah and Julia.

Tom Lynner has published poetry in *City View, Kentucky Review, River Oak Review* and *The North American Review*, and also enjoys working with the Des Moines National Poetry Festival which he co-founded. Born in Miami, he grew up in Des Moines, attended Cornell College and then went on to SUNY at Buffalo for his M.A. and Ph.D. He taught English at Drake University one year, and worked nights for three years in *The Des Moines Register* newsroom before leaving to become President of his family's real estate management business.

Debra Marquart teaches creative writing at Iowa State University in Ames. Her book of poetry, *Everything's a Verb*, won the Minnesota Voices Award and was published in 1995 by New Rivers Press. Currently Marquart is at work on a collection of short stories about road musicians entitled *Playing for the Door*, as well as a book of nonfictional essays about the Midwest entitled, *The Horizontal Life: Grim Tales from Dinky Towns.*

Ken McCullough's most recent books are *Travelling Light* (1987), and *Sycamore* (1991). His book *Plainsong* is scheduled for publication in 1996. He has received numerous awards for his poetry including the Academy of American Poets Award, a National Endowment for the Arts Fellowship, a Pablo Neruda Award, and the Capricorn Book Award. Most recently, he received a grant from the Witter Brynner Foundation for Poetry to continue translating the work of Cambodian poet U Sam Oeur, survivor of the Pol Pot concentration camps. McCullough and U are also working on U's autobiography and a chamber opera based on U's poems, as well as translation of Whitman's *Song of Myself* into the Khmer language.

James McKean was raised in the Seattle/Tacoma area and attended Washington State University. He received an M.F.A. and Ph.D. in English from the University of Iowa, and teaches at Mount Mercy College. His poems have appeared in the *The Atlantic, The Gettysburg Review,* and *Poetry.* In 1987 the University of Utah Press published his first book of poems, *Headlong,* which won the Great Lakes Colleges Association's New Writer Award. His second book, *Tree of Heaven,* won a 1994 Iowa Poetry Prize and was published in 1995 by the University of Iowa Press. He lives with his wife and daughter in Iowa City.

Sandra McPherson is the author of eight collections of poetry including: *The Spaces Between Birds: Mother/Daughter Poems 1967-1995* (Wesleyan, 1996), *Edge Effect: Trails and Portrayals* (Wesleyan, 1996), *The God of Indeterminacy* (Illinois, 1993), *Streamers* (Ecco, 1988), and *The Year of Our Birth* (Ecco, 1978), which was nominated for a National Book Award. Her honors and awards include two Ingram Merrill Foundation grants, three National Endowment for the Arts fellowships, and a Guggenheim fellowship. She was recently featured in a segment of *The Language of Life* with Bill Moyers. She has one daughter, Phoebe, and is married to the poet Walter Pavlich. All three of her poems in this collection were written in Iowa City.

Shaun Webb

Jane Mead's poems have been published widely in such places as *The American Poetry Review, Plowshares, The Boston Review, The New York Times*, and *The Best American Poetry of 1990*. In 1991 State Street Press published her long poem *A Truck Marked Flammable* as a chapbook. In 1992 she received a Whiting Writers' Award. In 1996 Sarabande Books published *The Lord and the General Din of the World*, which was chosen by Philip Levine as the winner of the Kathryn A. Morton Prize in Poetry.

Kim Westerman

Jane Miller's *Memory at These Speeds: New and Selected Poems* is forthcoming from Copper Canyon Press, which has also published her two previous collections, *American Odalisque* and *August Zero*. She has also written *Working Time: Essays on Poetry, Culture and Travel* (U. of Michigan). A recipient of a Lila Wallace-Reader's Digest Fund Award, a Guggenheim Fellowship, and two National Endowment for the Arts grants, she is Professor of English at The University of Arizona, currently on leave and living in San Francisco. She is a graduate of the University of Iowa's Writers' Workshop.

John Peterson was born and raised in northwest Iowa and attended the University of Iowa. He has worked as a social worker, a technician on off-shore oil rigs, and as a photographer and newspaper editor. He now lives in Kansas City, where he is completing work on a novel.

Keith Ratzlaff was born in Henderson, Nebraska and holds degrees from Bethel College in North Newton, Kansas and Indiana University. For the past 10 years he's taught writing and literature at Central College in Pella. His poems have appeared in numerous magazines and journals including *The Threepenny Review, Poetry Northwest,* and *The New England Review.* He's the author of two chapbooks: *Out Here* (State Street Press, 1984) and *New Winter Light* (Nightshade Press, 1994).

Dick Stahl was born in Davenport, Iowa. He received a B.A. from Augustana College (Rock Island, Illinois), an M.A. from the University of Iowa, and an Ed.S. from Western Illinois University. His first book, *After the Milk Route*, was published in 1988 by Augustana College's East Hall Press. His poems have appeared in the *English Journal, Farmer's Market, River Oak Review* and in the anthology *Forty Days and Forty Nights*. His second book, *Under the Green Tree Hotel*, will be published in the spring of 1996. He teaches English at Davenport Central High School.

Gerald Stern lived in Iowa from 1981 to 1995 and his presence there made a significant claim on his poetry both in terms of subject and spirit. He retired, in 1995, from his position as a permanent faculty member of the University of Iowa's Writers' Workshop. He is the author of nine books of poetry, the most recent being *Odd Mercy* (W.W. Norton). He is a native Pennsylvanian and currently lives in New York City and teaches at N.Y.U.

Meredith Stricker works in the fields of visual arts and poetry. She is a partner in Blue Design Studio, Iowa City and a current recipient of a 1995 Iowa Arts Council Artist Project Grant. Previous works were screened at the SF Poetry Film/Video Festival and are included in their permanent archives.

Her poetry has received Iowa Arts Council Literary Awards and the Montalvo Phelan Prize. *The Village Voice* writes: *"The past is reworked as ancestral languages and new languages meet. For Stricker, the linguistic search becomes an effort to regain all of our losses, 'the bee hum of all languages.'"*

Ann Struthers was born and grew up on an Iowa farm. She has published extensively in journals and is the author of two collections *Stoneboat* (Pterodactyl Press, 1988) and *The Alcott Family Arrives* (Coe Review Press, 1993). She is currently the Writer-in-Residence at Coe College in Cedar Rapids, Iowa.

Kim Stansbery

Jonathan Stull lives in Cedar Falls, Iowa with his wife Penny and his son Dylan. He has taught English for twenty years at Waterloo East High School, is a graduate of Upper Iowa University and The University of Iowa's Writers' Workshop. He has published poems in *Kansas Quarterly, The Wascana Review* and other literary magazines.

His book of poetry, *Singing the Lake's Desire*, is looking for a publisher.

Jon Van Allen

Mary Swander is the author of three books of poetry, *Heaven-and-Earth House* (Alfred Knopf, 1994), *Driving the Body Back* (Alfred Knopf, 1986), *Succession* (U. of Georgia Press, 1979), as well as a book of non-fiction *Parsnips in the Snow* (with Jane Staw, U. of Iowa Press, 1990). An edited collection of non-fiction and art work on the Loess Hills, *Land of the Fragile Giants* (with Cornelia Mutel, U. of Iowa Press) was published in 1994, and a memoir, *Out of this World*, was published by Viking in 1995. Ms. Swander adapted *Driving the Body Back* to the stage and this piece, along with her co-authored musical, *Dear Iowa* have been produced across the Midwest and on Iowa Public Television.

Ms. Swander has won numerous awards including a Whiting Award, the Carl Sandburg Literary Award, the Nation-Discovery Award, an NEA grant for the literary Arts and two Ingram Merrill Awards. She is professor of English at Iowa State University and lives in Ames and Kalona, Iowa, where she raises sheep and goats and a large organic garden.

Thom Swiss teaches at Drake University. His collection of poems, *Measure*, was published by the University of Alabama Press. Recent poems and essays appear in *Agni, Boston Review, The Iowa Review* and *Popular Music*.

Nicholas Tremmel

Robert Tremmel is from Sheldon in northwest Iowa. Educated at the University of Iowa, he is now an Associate Professor of English at Iowa State University. His first book *Driving the Milford Blacktop* was published in 1991 by BkMk Press. He has been published in numerous literary magazines and academic journals including: *Poetry Northwest, Kansas Quarterly, The Midwest Quarterly, Southern Poetry Review* and *Aethlon: The Journal of Sports Literature*.

Pat Underwood lives with her husband Steve along the North Skunk River in a former mining area outside Colfax, Iowa. She is an assistant preschool teacher, works part-time at a day-care facility and is an assistant editor of the Iowa Caregivers Association. Her work has recently appeared in *Poet & Critic, Opus Literary Review, Voices International, The Briar Cliff Review, Lyrical Iowa, Poetic Page* and *River King*. She has won awards in poetry from *Iowa Woman, Writer's Digest* and *NFSPS*.

Jan Weissmiller received an M.F.A. from the Iowa Writers' Workshop in 1984. She lives in Iowa City with her husband, the painter John Dilg, and has worked for many years at Prairie Lights Bookstore there. Her poems have previously appeared in *Pavement, River Styx* and *The Coe Review*.

Mary Jane White was born and raised in Charlotte, North Carolina. She has earned degrees from Reed College and The University of Iowa Writers' Workshop and studied law at Duke University and The University of Iowa. Her poetry and translations have received many awards, most recently N.E.A. Fellowships, in 1979 for her poetry and in 1985 for her translations. Her work has appeared in *The American Poetry Review, The Iowa Review, Crazy Horse* and *Russian Poetry: The Modern Period,* an anthology of translations. She practices law at her home in Waukon, Iowa, where she lives with her son Ruffin.

Sharen Barboza

Gary J. Whitehead, a 1994-95 Pearl Hogrefe Fellow in poetry at Iowa State University and a 1994 recipient of a Galway Kinnell Poetry Prize, is poetry editor of both *Flyway* and *Defined Providence*. His poems have recently appeared in *The Christian Science Monitor, Green Mountains Review, Southern Poetry Review* and *Yankee*. Originally from Providence, Rhode Island, he now lives in New Providence, Iowa with his wife Sharen, a psychologist.

Sidney Sander

Robley Wilson is a professor of English at the University of Northern Iowa, and since 1969 has edited *The North American Review*. His first poetry collection, *Kingdoms of the Ordinary*, won the 1986 Agnes Lynch Starrett prize; his second, *A Pleasure Tree*, the 1990 Society of Midland Authors poetry award. Wilson is also the author of four short-story collections and a novel. He is married to fiction writer Susan Hubbard.

Ray A. Young Bear is a lifetime resident of the Mesquakie (Red Earth) Tribal Settlement, outside Tama, Iowa. His poems have appeared in numerous anthologies and magazines including *American Poetry Review, Sulfur, Tri-Quarterly, The Georgia Review, The Kenyon Review, Shaking the Pumpkin, An Introduction to Poetry* and *Harper's Anthology of 20th Century Native American Poetry*. His first book of poetry, *Winter of the Salamander*, was published by Harper & Row. Young Bear has taught at the Institute of American Indian Arts, Eastern Washington University and The University of Iowa. Along with his spouse, Stella, he is also a singer and co-founder of the Woodland Song & Dance Troupe of Arts Midwest. In 1992, Young Bear published *Black Eagle Child: The Facepaint Narratives* (The University of Iowa Press). His fiction work *Remnants of the First Earth* will be published by Grove/Atlantic Monthly Press in 1996. He is currently working on *The Rock Island Hiking Club* (poems).

Michael Pettit

Paul Zimmer has published eleven books of poetry, including *Family Reunion* (U. of Pittsburgh Press, 1985), which won an Award for Literature from the American Academy and Institute of Arts and Letters; *The Great Bird of Love* (U. of Illinois Press, 1989); which was selected by William Stafford for the National Poetry Series; *Big Blue Train* (U. of Arkansas Press, 1993); and *Crossing to Sunlight: Selected Poems, 1965-1995*, which will be published by the U. of Georgia Press in the spring of 1996.

He has read his poems at close to 300 colleges and poetry centers from coast-to-coast, has recorded his poems for the Library of Congress, and has been awarded Writing Fellowships from the National Endowment for the Arts in 1974 and 1981. He has received three Pushcart Prizes and his poems have been widely anthologized. He was the Associate Director of the University of Pittsburgh Press (1967-1978), Director of the University of Georgia Press (1978-1984), and is currently Director of the University of Iowa Press.